Experiencing
the Passion
of Christ

✠

student edition

Experiencing the Passion of Christ

✠

student edition

John MacArthur

TRANSIT

Published by Nelson Impact, a Division of Thomas Nelson, Inc., P.O. Box 141000, Nashville, Tennessee, 37214.

Published in association with the literary agency of Wolgemuth & Associates, Inc.

Library of Congress Cataloging-in-Publication Data

MacArthur, John, 1939 –
  Experiencing the passion of Christ / by John MacArthur. — Student ed.
    p. cm.
  ISBN 1-4185-0342-8
  1. Jesus Christ — Passion — Study and teaching. 2. Jesus
Christ — Biography — Passion Week — Study and teaching. I. Title.
  BT431.3.M33 2005
  232.96 — dc22
                          2005004357

Printed in the United States of America.

05 06 07 – 9 8 7 6 5 4 3 2 1

Contents

Introduction

What a Sham!

Our culture is fascinated with court cases. We analyze the latest celebrity hearings on 20/20, 60 Minutes, or 48 Hours. We turn the life story of a gruesome murderer into People magazine fodder. We even have an entire cable channel devoted to broadcasting the judicial system's minute-by-minute workings. And in all this coverage, we're appalled when someone is tried for something he or she didn't do.

But this is nothing new. History is filled with famous cases of innocent victims who were wrongfully imprisoned or executed. And nowhere is this seen more graphically than in the arrest, trials, and crucifixion of Jesus Christ. No one was ever more innocent than the sinless Son of God. And yet no one ever suffered more agony than He did. He was cruelly executed by men who openly acknowledged His faultlessness while a murderous thief named Barabbas was set free in His place. It was the greatest travesty of justice the world will ever see.

Just look at the facts: Jesus Christ was the only sinless individual who ever lived—the most innocent, blameless, virtuous man of all time! He "committed no sin, nor was deceit found in His mouth" (1 Peter 2:22 NKJV). He was "holy, harmless, undefiled, separate from sinners" (Hebrews 7:26 NKJV). If anyone should've been rewarded and praised for his immaculate human existence, it was Jesus. And yet His reward on earth came in the form of the worst kind of torture, punishment, and death imaginable. No one has ever suffered more than He did, not just through physical pain, but also because of the spiritual torment. He bore the full weight of retribution for human evil. He suffered as if He were guilty of humanity's worst offenses. And yet He was guilty of nothing.

Who's in Control?

It's easy to look at the Cross and conclude that this was the worst miscarriage of human injustice in the history of the world. And it was. It was an evil act, perpetrated by the hands of wicked men. But that's not the *full* story.

The crucifixion of Christ was also the greatest act of divine justice ever carried out. This wasn't a human-conspired act. It was done in full accord with "the determined purpose and foreknowledge of God" (Acts 2:23 NKJV). Every harsh word and every lashing Jesus received was for the highest of purposes: to secure the salvation of untold numbers of people and open the way for God to forgive sin without compromising His own perfectly holy standard.

You're probably asking, "What does that mean?" We'll get into the details later in this book, but it basically boils down to this: God was in control. In order to save us from our naturally evil state so we could enjoy eternal fellowship with Him, a price had to be paid. Judgment had to come on the sin in the world. So when Christ hung on the cross, He wasn't a mere victim of a group of blood-thirsty savages. Sure, he was murdered unjustly and illegally by men whose intentions were only evil. But Christ died willingly, becoming the atonement for the sins of the same people who killed Him. It was the greatest sacrifice ever made, the purest act of love ever carried out, and ultimately, an infinitely higher act of divine justice than all the human *in*justice it represented.

A lot of people think Jesus was simply a casualty of human injustice, a martyr who suffered tragically and unnecessarily. But the truth is that His death was God's plan. In fact, it was the key to God's eternal plan of redemption. Far from being an unnecessary tragedy, the death of Christ was a glorious victory—the most gracious, kind, and wonderful act that sinners like you and I will ever know. It was the ultimate expression of God's love.

Swimming Deep

As Christians, we all know that Jesus died for our sins. That truth is so rich that only eternity will reveal its full implications. But we can often take the cross of Christ for granted as we coast through our day-to-day existence. Instead of seeing His ultimate sacrifice as an endless, majestic ocean, we treat it like a kiddie pool. Every once in a while, we'll dabble our toes in the shallow end and act as if we've had our fill of remembering what Christ did. The truth is, we should be swimming in the midst of huge waves every day, honoring what He did as a life-giving substance. We should be immersing ourselves daily in the water of His kindness.

That's what this book is for. It's about recalling what Christ really did, recounting every detail of His last hours, and taking in the full extent of God's extraordinary plan for our redemption.

So, are you ready to dive in?

Lesson 1

The Stage is Set

"Then the chief priests, the scribes, and the elders of the people assembled at the palace of the high priest, who was called Caiaphas, and plotted to take Jesus by trickery and kill Him."
—Matthew 26:3–4 NKJV

The Word to the Wise

Before starting this lesson, read John 11:47–50, 53 and Matthew 26:3–13.

For Starters

They'd had enough. The Jewish religious leaders might not have agreed on everything, but they knew one thing: this Jesus had to go. Who was this guy, anyway? He was just a carpenter's son from Galilee, yet He claimed to speak for God. He even had the nerve to say He was God's son. His radical sermons lured away people's hearts. He spoke with an authority only Pharisees and Sadducees should possess. He contradicted them, confounded them, and insulted them in their own synagogues. And with each week, the crowd following Jesus grew larger. He had to be silenced. He had to be stopped. He had to die.

Not Just a Conspiracy Theory

The drama of the Crucifixion begins in Matthew 26, where the plot to murder Jesus is hatched. A group of vengeful leaders gather to do more than whine to the high priest; they've started a conspiracy for His demise. They've waited long enough.

But so had Jesus. His entire life had led to this moment. Everything else had been a prologue. This was crunch time. Later, when He would stand before Pilate to be condemned to death, Christ Himself said, "For this cause I was born, and for this cause I have come into the world" (John 18:37 NKJV). He repeatedly spoke of the hour of His death as "My hour" (John 2:4; 7:6, 30; 8:20; 12:23; 13:1; 17:1 NKJV). Everything in His life was preparation for the hour of His death.

Jesus wasn't fooled by the religious leaders' trickery and deception. They may have plotted in secrecy, but Jesus knew it was all part of the bigger picture. His final hour had come. The scheming of men coincided with God's divine purposes.

> Rejoice greatly, O daughter of Zion! Shout, O daughter of Jerusalem! Behold, your King is coming to you; He is just and having salvation, Lowly and riding on a donkey, A colt, the foal of a donkey.
>
> —Zechariah 9:9 NKJV

1. If Jesus knew His biggest accomplishment was to die, why do you think He agreed to become a man in the first place? (Check out Jesus' words in John 12:27.)

_____

_____

_____

To what degree did Jesus humble Himself by becoming a man, according to Philippians 2:5–8?

_____

_____

_____

What does Hebrews 2:14 say was the ultimate purpose of Jesus' death?

_____

_____

_____

They didn't care if Jesus was the true Messiah or not; they wanted Him gone.

The Jewish leaders were scared stiff of Jesus. His rising popularity could potentially lead to people calling Him the Messiah, which could then result in pressure to recognize Him as the rightful ruler of the Jews. And that was bad news. Any rising force among the Jews was a threat to the high priest and Sanhedrin, who were pawns to the ruling Roman government (John 11:48). If they didn't silence this Jesus talk and squelch the messianic rumors, their jobs—and lives—would be in danger. They didn't care if Jesus was the true Messiah or not; they wanted Him gone.

2. What drove the Jewish leaders to the point of wanting Jesus dead?

_____

_____

_____

The religious leaders felt threatened by Jesus. He was popular; they weren't. But popularity is fleeting. Only days before, Jesus had been the main attraction of a parade in his honor. He'd ridden into the city in triumph while shouts of "Hosanna" rang from crowds lining the streets. Obviously, He was destined to be swept onto the throne with an unstoppable wave of grassroots support, right?

3. As Jesus rode into Jerusalem, the Pharisees watched from a distance. John 12:19 says they admitted they were "accomplishing nothing. Look, the world has gone after Him!" (NKJV). What does their comment say about their motives?

_____

_____

_____

DON'T BELIEVE THE HYPE

Most of us would've soaked up such flattery and praise, but Jesus knew the real truth. Public opinion is fickle. People may say you're the greatest one day and spread rumors about you the next. As the ultimate truth, Jesus knew He had to walk an unpopular path regardless of the word on the street. The fawning masses may have been attracted to Jesus' miracles, but they weren't ready to acknowledge their sin and truly follow Him. In fact, many of the same people who were shouting hosannas to Him at the beginning of the week were yelling "Crucify Him, crucify Him!" before the week was over.

> He is despised and rejected by men, a Man of sorrows and acquainted with grief.
>
> —Isaiah 53:3 NKJV

Fair Warning

Jesus had warned His disciples several times that He would die at the hands of those who hated Him. In fact, long before His final journey to Jerusalem, "while they were staying in Galilee, Jesus said to them, 'The Son of Man is about to be betrayed into the hands of men, and they will kill Him'" (Matt. 17:22–23 NKJV).

Now the hour had come, and an unstoppable chain of events had begun that would end in His murder. His final week of earthly ministry was drawing to a close. Christ had just given His disciples an incredible series of lessons on the Mount of Olives (Matt. 24–25). But it's obvious that His thoughts were on more than parables and sermon illustrations. He was about to die and He knew it. Matthew writes, "Now it came to pass, when Jesus had finished all these sayings, that He said to His disciples, 'You know that after two days is the Passover, and the Son of Man will be delivered up to be crucified'" (Matt. 26:1–2 NKJV). The time for teaching was up; His time for dying was at hand. The sovereign plan of God for the redemption of all humanity was about to come to fruition. And although evil men were at that very moment plotting His death in secret, it was no secret to the sovereign, all-knowing God.

4. This wasn't the first time Jesus' enemies had sought to kill Him. Remember these thwarted attempts on Christ's life? Who tried to kill Jesus in each case, and why?

Matthew 2:13

_____

_____

_____

Luke 4:28–29

_____

_____

_____

John 5:18

_____

_____

_____

> We hid, as it were, our faces from Him.
>
> —Isaiah 53:3 NKJV

During Jesus' earlier days of ministry, it became so well known that the Jewish leaders were after His life that the buzz on the Jerusalem streets labeled Him as "He whom they seek to kill" (John 7:25 NKJV). But the death threats didn't faze Him one bit. Jesus fearlessly went about His business of speaking boldly to the masses. The Jewish leaders, on the other hand, were intimidated by His courage and said nothing to Him. Their avoidance ended up backfiring on them, as people began to wonder if the Sanhedrin knew He was the Messiah (John 7:26). Even the temple guard assigned to arrest Him cowered at His boldness. And when the chief priests and Pharisees demanded to know why He hadn't been arrested, the temple officers couldn't help but admit, "No man ever spoke like this Man!" (John 7:46 NKJV). Clearly, His words had power.

It didn't matter what the schemers tried; it wasn't Jesus' time yet, at least not until the Father said so.

5. Why were Jesus' words so powerful?

_____

_____

_____

The Ringleader

One man became the central figure in the plot to kill Jesus: Caiaphas, the high priest that year. Caiaphas was a politically motivated, hard-nosed opportunist. In other words, he was shady, someone who would say or do anything just to make himself look better.

In the Old Testament, high priests were direct descendents of Aaron. They were called Levites. But during Rome's occupation of the Jewish nation, the Roman government decided who would be high priest. Historical evidence strongly suggests that the office was often bought with money or granted as a political favor. Forget righteousness; it was all about who could offer the most.

Caiaphas found his way in by marrying the daughter of Annas, a former high priest (John 18:13). Annas still held significant power through his son-in-law, so it became a two-headed priesthood of sorts (Luke 3:2). History books indicate that this lasted for more than twenty years, which meant Caiaphas had somehow gained unusual favor with Rome. But history doesn't stop there. It also speaks of Caiaphas's corruption: He was the high priest responsible for allowing money changers into the temple. (He no doubt got a fat cut of their sales, making him slimy *and* rich.) Since it was Jesus who twice drove away these merchants from the temple (John 2:14–16; Matt. 21:12–13), it's no surprise that Caiaphas wanted Him out of the picture.

Despite Caiaphas's hatred for Jesus, he fit right into God's plan. At one point, the high priest announced, "It is expedient for us that one man should die for the people, and not that the whole nation should perish" (John 11:50 NKJV). While the scheming high priest was speaking directly about murdering Jesus to save his own hide by squelching a political threat, God had other intentions. John noticed this when he commented on Caiaphas's remarks: "Now this he did not say on his own authority; but being high priest that year he prophesied that Jesus would die for the nation, and not for that nation only, but also that He would gather together in one the children of God who were scattered abroad" (John 11:51–52 NKJV).

Prophecy from the very guy who plotted Christ's death? Only God had a plan so wonderfully upside-down.

6. Caiaphas's impure motives led to the sacrifice that redeemed the world. Something similar happened to Joseph back in the Old Testament. Though his older brothers had nothing but murder in mind, God used their evil schemes to save their whole family. How did Joseph sum it up in Genesis 50:20?

_____

_____

_____

In other words, what Caiaphas and the Sanhedrin were planning for evil reasons, God intended for good. They wanted to kill Jesus to preserve their prestige and political position. But God allowed His Son to be sacrificed so a nation—people from *every* nation—could be saved from a rightful sentencing of death. Rather than let us suffer the consequences of our sinfulness, He let His Son do it. "He Himself is the propitiation for our sins, and not for ours only but also for the whole world"

> Despite Caiaphas's hatred for Jesus, he fit right into God's plan.

(1 John 2:2 NKJV). The schemers' evil plans were made to kill Jesus, but God's wonderful plan was to save the world in the process.

Time's Up

Jesus knew when it was His time. On the night of His arrest, He told the disciples, "The Son of Man goes as it has been determined" (Luke 22:22 NKJV). Once again, He wasn't surprised by a single move of His enemies.

Notice that the scheme of the Sanhedrin was "to take Jesus by trickery and kill Him. But they said, 'Not during the feast, lest there be an uproar among the people'"(Matt. 26:4–5 NKJV). It's obvious these guys wanted to kill Christ with as little fanfare as possible. Because of that, they decided to wait until the Passover season was over so Jerusalem wouldn't be so crowded. They weren't trying to be holy by not killing during the feast. In fact, criminals were often executed during the feasts because there were more witnesses at those times. No, instead these religious leaders wanted to do their deed in the dark. They wanted to remain secretive so they wouldn't provoke a public uproar.

Yet again, God was in control even over this. They wanted to avoid a public scandal on the feast day; God's design was for Christ to die on Passover, in as public a manner as possible. Guess who won out?

7. What does Proverbs 19:21 say about the schemes of men compared to the plans of God?

_____

_____

_____

Jerusalem was the major hot spot during the Passover. People from all over the Roman Empire came to the city to celebrate the season. Even Roman governor Pontius Pilate (whose headquarters were in the coastal town of Caesarea) came. Obviously, if the Jewish religious leaders wanted to quietly seize and kill Jesus, this was the worst time—and place—to do it. Once word got out among Jesus' supporters of His arrest, a riot seemed imminent.

But Passover was His time—the time God had chosen, the time most fitting for the Lamb of God to die for the sins of the world. And the conspiracy would ultimately be carried out according to God's timing, not Caiaphas's. When the conspirators had tried to kill Jesus in the past, God had thwarted their plans. Now the tables were turned: despite wanting to delay the timing of Jesus' death, God had the final say-so.

> But Passover was His time—the time God had chosen, the time most fitting for the Lamb of God to die for the sins of the world.

DID YA KNOW?

The historian Josephus estimated that more than a quarter million sacrificial lambs would be slain in Jerusalem during a typical Passover season. On average, ten people would account for one lamb, meaning that the Jewish population in Jerusalem during Passover could swell to between 2.5 and 3 million.

> It is expedient for us that one man should die for the people, and not that the whole nation should perish.
>
> —John 11:50 NKJV

8. The religious leaders didn't just have a grudge against Jesus. They despised Him to the core. They spent most of His public life trying to corner Him and discredit His teaching with trick questions. The more He refuted their claims, the more their hatred grew. But this was expected; it had been prophesied in the Old Testament and confirmed by Jesus Himself. Match the following Scriptures with the appropriate prophesies and statements.

___ Isaiah 53:3   a. Jesus taught that He would be rejected by religious leaders.

___ Mark 8:31   b. Those who hated Jesus also hated the Father.

___ Mark 13:13   c. The Messiah was despised and rejected by men.

___ Luke 17:25   d. Jesus, the rejected stone, was chosen by God and precious.

___ John 15:18   e. Jesus would first suffer and be rejected by His generation.

___ John 15:24   f. They hated Jesus without a cause to do so.

___ John 15:25   g. We'll also be hated for His name's sake.

___ 1 Peter 2:4   h. We are hated because the world first hated Jesus.

Preparing the Body

It seems kind of odd: Right after beginning to relay the events of Christ's Passion Week, Matthew stops to tell the story of Mary. Not Mary, Jesus' mother, but Mary, the sister of Martha and Lazarus. Remember her? Whenever Jesus was around, she'd sit at His feet and soak up His every word. She'd spend every moment she could talking with Him, listening to Him, and simply enjoying His presence.

Here, Matthew pauses amid the trials and looming suffering of Jesus to remind us of who He really is and what He really deserves. The moment when Mary anoints Jesus' feet stands in stark contrast to the conspiracy being plotted in the palace of the high priest. There, men who hated Jesus plotted His demise. Here, a woman who loved Jesus lavishes Him with love and honor while symbolically (and unknowingly) preparing Him for burial.

This wasn't just your average twenty-five-dollar perfume. Both John 12:5 and Mark 14:5 record that the ointment was worth three hundred denarii—about a year's wages for the typical worker. And Mary had a *pound* of this stuff! It came in an alabaster flask, also a pricey thing. Mark records that Mary broke the flask (Mark 14:3), which makes her sacrificial act even more extreme. She wasn't going to spend an ounce of this stuff on anything or anyone but Jesus.

But check out the disciples' reactions. They were outraged over Mary's "wastefulness." She wasn't just dabbing this on Jesus' feet; she was *pouring* it on. Someone had probably donated or spent a lot of money purchasing that perfume. The disciples could've sold it and given the proceeds to the poor. In fact, Judas was the first to voice this complaint to the other disciples. What a thoughtful guy, right?

John is quick to squelch any honorable thoughts about Judas's words: "This he said, not that he cared for the poor, but because he was a thief, and had the money box; and he used to take what was put in it" (John 12:6 NKJV). It's important to note that Judas was the group's treasurer. He was trusted (Ps. 41:9), and the fact that the others followed his lead in complaining about Mary's actions reveals that he had gained not only their trust but also their respect. Obviously, they never suspected that Judas would become a traitor, because even when Jesus prophesied that He would be betrayed by one of them, not one person pointed the finger at Judas. They all seemed to doubt themselves more than they doubted Judas (Mark 14:19).

> "But as for you, you meant evil against me; but God meant it for good, in order to bring it about as it is this day, to save many people alive."
>
> —Genesis 50:20 NKJV

9. Picture yourself as a disciple watching Mary douse Jesus' feet with perfume. In all honesty, what would your first reaction be?

_____

_____

_____

If Judas came to you complaining that the perfume could've been better used, what would you say?

_____

_____

_____

Why were the disciples not the least bit suspicious of Judas?

_____

_____

_____

In typical Judas fashion, the eventual traitor didn't voice his displeasure about Mary's act in front of Jesus. According to Mark, the disciples first discussed the matter privately among themselves, and then they took their complaint—framed as a sharp rebuke—to Mary (Mark 14:4–5). Again, how thoughtful of them not to embarrass her in front of Jesus, right? Hardly. Jesus knew their concerns, even though they hadn't voiced them. And He quickly rebuked them for not getting the point: "Let her alone" (John 12:7 NKJV) . . . "For in pouring this fragrant oil on My body, she did it for My burial" (Matt. 26:12 NKJV).

Mary's gesture of love and worship to Christ was a divinely ordained symbolic act of preparation for His death and burial. In those days, bodies were prepared for burial using perfumes and ointments. Mary had no clue Christ would soon be literally buried in a tomb, but God did. And Jesus recognized that this, in a sense, was a token of love from His Father to Him, signifying that now was His time.

A Done Deal

Judas was sick of it. This last reprimanding from Jesus probably sealed the deal. It's possible that Judas's disillusionment with his teacher had been growing beforehand. Maybe Jesus really wasn't the Messiah. After all, wasn't the real Redeemer supposed to deliver Israel from Roman oppression? Wasn't He supposed to come down through heavenly clouds and ascend the throne as king? Judas (as well as other disciples) no doubt had hoped to share in the glory and power of that kingdom (Matt. 20:20–21). But all this talk from Jesus about rejection, suffering, and His impending death was simply a downer. What kind of savior would tell His disciples to hush every time they wanted to give Him a little PR push?

Judas had hung around Jesus for three years now, and he was tired of waiting for this guy to take the throne of David. Furthermore, he was tired of waiting to see if Jesus would promote him as top money man in this new kingdom. Something told him there was a faster way to success.

And so in this thirst for power, Judas came up with another plan. He needed fast cash. Apparently, stealing from the disciples' treasury wasn't cutting it. He couldn't watch another pound of spikenard be wasted when that could've been another dollar in his own pocket. As Judas saw the potential profits of a planned embezzlement evaporate, he may have decided then and there to make up for the loss by selling Jesus. Maybe this "Messiah" was worth something after all.

10. Judas often gets the wrong press. He wasn't a weak-minded disciple, lured aside and trapped into treachery by the wiles of the Sanhedrin. In fact, it was Judas who approached them with the offer to betray his Master. What proposition did Judas make, according to Matthew 26:15?

_____

_____

_____

The Bible has some words of warning to those who, like Judas, are consumed with a love for money. What does 1 Timothy 6:10 say will happen to those obsessed with the big buck?

_____

_____

_____

> The Pharisees therefore said among themselves, "You see that you are accomplishing nothing. Look, the world has gone after Him!"
>
> —John 12:19 NKJV

WAS JUDAS JUST A TOOL?

How do we reconcile the fact that Judas's treachery was prophesied and predetermined with the fact that he acted of his own volition? It's a good question. But actually, there's no need to reconcile those two facts because they're not contradictory. Judas did what he did because his heart was evil. He wasn't coerced into doing what he did. No invisible hand forced him to betray Christ. He acted freely out of a heart that had turned bitter toward Jesus. On the other hand, God, who works all things according to the counsel of His own will (Eph. 1:11), had foreordained that Jesus would be betrayed and that He would die for the sins of the world. Both things are true. The perfect will of God and the wicked purposes of Judas coincided to bring about Christ's death. There's no contradiction. —*Twelve Ordinary Men*

The moment Judas turned from Christ, he willingly gave himself over to the control of the powers of darkness and became a tool of Satan.

Luke records that Satan himself entered into Judas at about this time (Luke 22:3). Operating through Judas's greed, and taking advantage of a rebellious heart that had by now given up on Jesus, the devil literally possessed Judas to carry out the act of treachery about to occur. The moment Judas turned from Christ, he willingly gave himself over to the control of the powers of darkness and became a tool of Satan.

Judas knew his teacher was worth something. His treacherous plans perfectly melded with those of Caiaphas—but only if the price was right. The high priest and his cohorts agreed to the betrayal price: thirty pieces of silver (Matt. 26:15), which was also the price of a slave. In one deal, Judas had sold his Lord and his soul, eternally making himself a slave to darkness. Interestingly enough, Judas was probably paid in silver shekels. Thirty shekels would be worth about 120 denarii—less than the value of Mary's spikenard.

For Judas, it was go-time. He had accepted the money and was committed to the deal. Now he had to wait for the prime opportunity to betray Jesus, a time when his teacher was alone so that the Sanhedrin could capture Him quietly. And Judas knew just the place.

11. That evening's stroll wasn't the first time Jesus and His disciples walked along the paths of the Garden of Gethsemane. How does John describe the place in John 18:2?

_____

_____

_____

Wrapping It Up

From an earthly perspective, it appeared that the schemes of Jesus' enemies were coming together perfectly. The Sanhedrin had a spy in Jesus' inner circle of friends. The price had been paid, and the conspiracy's groundwork had been laid. Things were falling together nicely. Or so it seemed.

A plot was definitely underway, but it wasn't the plot that the enemy was expecting. A higher plan had taken advantage of their petty scheming. It was the eternal plan of a sovereign God—a plan that had been laid out from before the foundation of the world.

Things to Remember

❦ Jesus spoke of the hour of His death as "My hour." It was why He had come.
❦ With the public's recent adoration of Jesus, it seemed as if He'd be swept onto the Messianic throne with an unstoppable wave of grassroots support.
❦ A chain of events had begun that would end in the murder of Jesus.
❦ What Caiaphas and the Sanhedrin were planning for evil reasons, God intended for good.
❦ Money-hungry, politically ambitious Judas had hoped to share in the glory and power as one of Messiah's inner circle.
❦ A plot was definitely underway, but it wasn't the plot that the enemy was expecting.

Memorize This!

Let this mind be in you which was also in Christ Jesus, who, being in the form of God, did not consider it robbery to be equal with God, but made Himself of no reputation, taking the form of a bondservant, and coming in the likeness of men. And being found in appearance as a man, He humbled Himself and became obedient to the point of death, even the death of the cross.

—Philippians 2:5–8 NKJV

It was the eternal plan of a sovereign God—a plan that had been laid out from before the foundation of the world.

Check This Out

If you want to find out more about the following related topics, check out John MacArthur's extensive resources in the *MacArthur LifeWorks Library CD-ROM*, or visit www.gty.org.

✠ Tension between Jesus and the religious leaders
✠ The Triumphal Entry
✠ Mary's anointing of Jesus' feet with perfume
✠ Judas's greed
✠ Thirty pieces of silver
✠ God's sovereignty in the midst of apparent chaos
✠ The people's expectations about Messiah

Lesson 2
One Last Meal

"My time is at hand; I will keep the Passover . . . with My disciples."
—Matthew 26:18 NKJV

The Word to the Wise

Before starting this lesson, read Matthew 26:17–30.

For Starters

There's a buzz about holidays, especially when it comes to Christmas. Every year, we celebrate God's gift to earth with carols, lights, decorations, trees, parties, eggnog, and (your favorite part) gifts. It's a magical time for families.

For Jews during Jesus' time, Passover had a similar buzz. It was a holiday filled with tradition, celebration, reunion, and thanksgiving. Crowds of people poured into Jerusalem—the Holy City—every year to thank God for His faithfulness and to celebrate God's provision of freedom. Families spent time together preparing for the festivities, rolling out the unleavened bread for baking, stirring fruit and spices into the sweet *charoseth*, washing the bitter herbs, and, out of tradition, setting the table with an extra spot, in case Elijah should come. Parents gathered their children around to tell stories of generations past, while the history of a chosen nation was revered by all.

It was on Passover that Jesus gathered His closest friends for His last meal. He welcomed the company, because this was a bittersweet time for Him. He'd grown up coming to Jerusalem for the Passover each year with Mary and Joseph (Luke 2:41). They would go to the temple to sacrifice a lamb, and Jesus would watch the blood pour down the city streets. But in just a few hours, the city would be sprinkled—immersed—with *His* dying blood.

> It was on Passover that Jesus gathered His closest friends for His last meal.

It's a Holy Day

Passover was the first feast of the Jewish calendar, held every year "on the fourteenth day of the first month at twilight" (Lev. 23:5 NKJV). It had been observed in Israel since the eve of the Jews' departure from Egypt under Moses—almost fifteen hundred years before Christ. It was the oldest of the Old Covenant rituals, even older than the priesthood, the tabernacle, and the rest of the Mosaic sacrificial system. On that holy day, every family in Israel commemorated their nation's deliverance from slavery in Egypt with the sacrifice of a spotless lamb.

1. Passover wasn't just a manmade holiday; it was appointed by God. Read Exodus 12:13–27.

_____

_____

_____

How did Passover get its name?

_____

_____

_____

What sign had to be present for God to pass over a house?

_____

_____

_____

What happened in the houses that God didn't pass over but actually went through?

_____

_____

_____

> When I see the blood, I will pass over you; and the plague shall not be on you to destroy you when I strike the land of Egypt.
>
> —Exodus 12:13 NKJV

Four days before Passover, every family in Israel was to select a spotless, sacrificial lamb and separate that lamb from the rest of the herds until Passover, when the lamb was to be killed (Ex. 12:3–6). During that final week before His Crucifixion, Jesus most likely did this with His disciples, choosing a lamb on Monday of that week.

2. God wasn't into just any ordinary lamb serving as a sacrifice. Fill in the following blanks to find what qualities God required for a Passover lamb.

Exodus 12:5 — "Your lamb shall be _____ _____"(NKJV).

Leviticus 22:21 — "Whoever offers a _____ of a peace offering to the LORD . . . from the cattle or the _____, it must be _____ to be _____; there shall be no _____ in it" (NKJV).

Deuteronomy 17:1— "You shall not _____ to the LORD your God a bull or _____ which has any _____ or _____, for that is an _____ to the LORD your God" (NKJV).

3. The idea of being spotless and without blemish carries over into the New Testament. Match up the following Scriptures that apply this high standard to believers.

___ Ephesians 5:27   a. Keep God's commandments, without spot and blemish.

___ 1 Timothy 6:14   b. Be diligent to be found without spot and blameless.

___ Hebrews 9:14   c. The church will be presented without spot or wrinkle.

___ 1 Peter 1:19   d. Jesus' offering was spotless, and His blood cleanses us.

___ 2 Peter 3:14   e. Jesus' precious blood was like that of a perfect lamb.

✠

DID YA KNOW?

The Jews of Jesus' day had two different methods of marking days on the calendar. The Pharisees, along with the Jews from the north and Galilee, counted their days from sunrise to sunrise. The Sadducees, along with the people from Jerusalem and the surrounding area, calculated days from sundown to sundown. That meant that 14 Nisan for a Galilean fell on Thursday, while 14 Nisan for Jerusalem folk fell on Friday. This allowed the slaughter of lambs at the temple to take place over the course of two evenings.

✠

> Your lamb shall be without blemish.
>
> —Exodus 12:5 NKJV

Historical records of Jesus' time indicate that as many as a quarter million lambs were slain in a typical Passover season. All that slaughtering required hundreds of priests to carry out the task. Since all the lambs were killed during a two-hour period just before twilight on 14 Nisan (Ex. 12:6), it would have required about six hundred priests, killing an average of four lambs per minute, to accomplish the task in a single evening! Fortunately, the process was spread out over two evenings, giving the priests a little more breathing room.

Still, there was a ton of blood spilled from these sacrifices, as you can imagine. In fact, Jewish law permitted the blood's flow from the steep eastern slope of the temple mount into the Kidron Valley, where it turned the brook bright crimson for a period of several days. It was a massive—and graphic—reminder of the awful price of sin.

But here's the sad truth: all the blood from all those animals and all the animals since still isn't enough to remedy our sin problem. When God set the world in order, He declared the penalty of sin to be death. Think of all the evil thoughts, actions, and motives you've already had today. It would take a lot of lambs to make up for your sin. Now think of all the people in your city . . . your state . . . the United States . . . even the world! We'd probably run out of lambs. And that's just making up for one day's worth of sin!

The Bible says it clearly: "For it is not possible that the blood of bulls and goats could take away sins" (Heb. 10:4 NKJV). God knew that, and so He made the lamb's killing to symbolize a more perfect sacrifice that would eventually take away all sins. John the Baptist knew who this was: Jesus. He called Him the true "Lamb of God who takes away the sin of the world" (John 1:29 NKJV). But most everyone else during Jesus' life didn't catch on to this. They would soon discover the full meaning of John's words.

4. Paul refers to Jesus in 1 Corinthians 5:7 as "our Passover" (NKJV). Why do Christians still consider Christ as the sacrificial lamb for a distinctly Jewish holiday?

_____

_____

_____

> Indeed Christ, our Passover, was sacrificed for us.
>
> —1 Corinthians 5:7 NKJV

> "For it is not possible that the blood of bulls and goats could take away sins."
>
> —Hebrews 10:4 NKJV

Time to Prepare

It was early Thursday morning. The disciples were as giddy as kids waking up on December 25. Passover was here, and preparations were in order for the meal. Now all they needed was a place to eat: "Now on the first day of the Feast of Unleavened Bread the disciples came to Jesus, saying to Him, 'Where do You want us to prepare for You to eat the Passover?'" (Matt. 26:17 NKJV).

Evidently, Jesus had already made arrangements for the evening meal. In those days, it was common for Jerusalem residents to rent out their spare rooms to people coming into town for the festivities. Jesus had reserved a spot for Himself and the disciples—an upper room. But He had secretly made these preparations to avoid having it known in advance where He would be that evening. It ensured their privacy, but it also kept Judas from revealing Jesus' location to the Sanhedrin. Jesus wanted to have one last quiet meal with His disciples. He had some important things to tell them.

Peter and John were put in charge of preparing the Upper Room. On several other occasions, the two had heard Jesus say, "My time has not yet come" (John 7:6 NKJV)—or words to that effect. His time was now at hand. He was counting down to the moment for which He had come into the world. Jesus knew He had one remaining evening to spend with His disciples, and He would spend it keeping the Passover.

TIME CHANGE

Some people are confused by the different Gospel accounts of when the Last Supper took place and when Jesus was crucified. Matthew, Mark, and Luke all describe Jesus eating with His disciples on Thursday evening and then being crucified on Friday. But John seemingly mixes things up by stating that Jesus' trial and crucifixion were on the day of preparation for the Passover and not after the eating of the Passover (John 19:14). What gives?

The answer lies again in the two ways that Jews kept track of days. Being Galileans (northerners), Jesus and the disciples considered Passover day to have started at sunrise on Thursday and ended at sunrise on Friday. The Jewish leaders who arrested and tried Jesus, being mostly priests and Sadducees, considered Passover day to begin at sunset on Thursday and end at sunset on Friday. This explains how Jesus could celebrate the last Passover meal with His disciples and yet still be sacrificed on Passover day—yet another fulfillment of an Old Testament prophecy.

A Final Lesson

"When evening had come, He sat down with the twelve" (Matt. 26:20 NKJV). It would have been after 6:00 on Thursday evening when they sat down to the meal. There was a specific order to follow for the Passover seder. A cup of wine was distributed first, the first of four cups shared during the meal. Each person would take a sip from a common cup. Before the cup was passed, Jesus gave thanks (Luke 22:17).

After the initial cup was passed, there was a ceremonial washing to symbolize the need for moral and spiritual cleansing. It's at this point when things get a little silly for the disciples. Here they are at a crucial point in Christ's life—one that will be remembered through paintings and writings for thousands of years—and they begin arguing about "which of them should be considered the greatest" (Luke 22:24 NKJV). Most of us wouldn't have known whether to laugh or cry at the situation. But Jesus, as always, turns it into a life-altering learning point for His friends. John records that Jesus "rose from supper and laid aside His garments, took a towel and girded Himself. After that, He poured water into a basin and began to wash the disciples' feet, and to wipe them with the towel with which He was girded" (John 13:4–5 NKJV).

Footwashing was normally done by the lowest servant. It definitely wasn't something the disciples expected Jesus—their Teacher, Mentor, and Master—to do for them. Yet He used the opportunity to show them the true meaning of humility and holiness. His actions reiterated something He'd probably said to them a thousand

Footwashing was normally done by the lowest servant. It definitely wasn't something the disciples expected Jesus—their Teacher, Mentor, and Master—to do for them.

My time is at hand; I will keep the Passover at your house with My disciples.

—Matthew 26:18 NKJV

times: "Whoever desires to become great among you, let him be your servant" (Matt. 20:26 NKJV).

5. Jesus' last object lesson to the future leaders of the Christian church was one of servanthood and humility.

Why do you think these qualities were so important to Jesus?

_____

_____

_____

According to James 4:10, what should our attitude be?

_____

_____

_____

In 1 Peter 5:5–6, what does the apostle tell us will happen when we humble ourselves before the Lord?

_____

_____

_____

> The Son of Man did not come to be served, but to serve, and to give His life a ransom for many.
>
> —Matthew 20:28 NKJV

6. What are Jesus' words as He leaves these men with such a memorable lesson of humility? Fill in the blanks of Luke 22:27 (NKJV):

"I am _____ you as the _____ who _____."

—— ✠ ——

DID YA KNOW?

Footwashing was a task typically delegated to the lowest slave. It removed the dust, mud, and other filth encountered on the unpaved roads in and around Jerusalem. Normally in a hired banquet room like this, an attendant would be provided to wash guests' feet when they entered. But evidently there was no servant to perform the task when Jesus and the disciples arrived. Instead of humbling themselves to perform such a demeaning task for one another, the disciples had simply left their feet unwashed. Christ's gesture was both a touching act of self-abasement and a subtle rebuke to the disciples (John 13:6–9).

—— ✠ ——

After the ceremonial washing, the Passover meal continued by eating bitter herbs (Ex. 12:8)—parsley, endive, and similar leafy greens. These were taken to remember the horrible years of Israel's bondage in Egypt. The herbs were eaten with pieces of unleavened bread (bread that hasn't risen), dipped in a substance called *charoseth*, a chutney made of pomegranates, apples, dates, figs, raisins, and vinegar. The pasty *charoseth* represented a bricklayer's mortar—and again it was reminiscent of the Israelites' slavery in Egypt, where they made bricks.

Next, the second cup was passed. This would be accompanied by the singing of psalms. Traditionally, the psalms sung at Passover were from the Hallel—six psalms beginning with Psalm 113. The first two were sung at this point in the ceremony. The roasted lamb would be served next, along with pieces of the unleavened bread.

Dinner Gone Sour

Have you ever sat next to someone who delivered a real conversation-stopper at a meal? You know, a statement that quiets the whole table and makes everything from that moment on seem drenched in awkwardness?

Jesus probably pulled one of these at this point in the Passover meal. Everything was fine—somber, but still fine. The disciples were gratefully reflecting on God's faithfulness to Israel. But Jesus saw fit to deliver the whopper at this point. "Now as they were eating, He said, 'Assuredly, I say to you, one of you will betray Me'" (Matt. 26:21 NKJV).

Remember, Jesus had mentioned His coming death many times previously, though it usually went right over His disciples' heads. But this was the first time He'd said anything about being betrayed by one of His own disciples. Talk about being a party-pooper! Here the disciples had been in such a festive mood, and Jesus drops the hammer by saying one of His best friends would turn his back on Him. What's interesting, however, is Matthew's recollection of the disciples' response. "They were exceedingly sorrowful, and each of them began to say to Him, 'Lord, is it I?'" (Matt. 26:22 NKJV).

It seemed unimaginable to most of the disciples that one of them would give Jesus over to His enemies. And yet their response—"Who, me?"—shows that they realized the potential in their hearts for such treachery. Things were getting tense. The air seemed heavier. The silence grew thicker.

Jesus finally spoke, but He didn't allay their fears. Instead, He simply underscored the hideous nature of the treason that was about to take place by saying, "He who dipped his hand with Me in the dish will betray Me" (Matt. 26:23 NKJV).

7. How does Psalm 55:12–14 describe the pain of such hypocrisy and betrayal? Fill in the blanks of David's psalm here.

For it is not an _____ who _____ me;

Then I could _____ it.

Nor is it one who _____ me who has _____ himself against me;

I am among you as the One who serves.

—Luke 22:27 NKJV

Then I could _____ from him.

But it was _____, a man my _____,

My _____ and my _____.

We took _____ _____ together,

and _____ to the _____ of _____ in

the_____(NKJV).

> "Lord, who is it?" Jesus answered, "It is he to whom I shall give a piece of bread when I have dipped it."
>
> —John 13:25–26 NKJV

In Psalm 41:9, David wrote a similar lament about his trusted counselor, Ahithophel, who joined Absalom's rebellion against David: "Even my own familiar friend in whom I trusted, who ate my bread, has lifted up his heel against me" (NKJV).

The eleven disciples besides Judas were appalled by the thought that one of them would be guilty of such a sinister act. And yet their first response wasn't finger-pointing but self-examination. No doubt they were still reeling introspectively from their lack of humility shown when their own Master washed their feet. "Why didn't I think of that?" they were probably saying to themselves. Yet it showed them their own sinful frailty. And now they were confronted with something even more troubling.

Am I the one? Could I be the person Jesus is talking about? I'd never do anything to harm Him . . . but maybe I've done something to put Him in jeopardy. You can hear their thoughts. They're kicking themselves, racking their brains to remember if at some point—*any* point—they accidentally gave Jesus away to His enemies.

John records, "The disciples looked at one another, perplexed about whom He spoke" (John 13:22 NKJV). There was nothing in either Judas's behavior or Jesus' treatment of him up to this point that would've given the other disciples a clue that Judas was the betrayer. Although "Jesus knew from the beginning who they were who did not believe, and who would betray Him" (John 6:64 NKJV), He had never been reserved or withdrawn from Judas; He had always treated him with the same tenderness and goodwill He'd shown the others. In fact, Judas's role as treasurer seemed to indicate an extra level of trust Jesus had for him. He was probably one of the last disciples anyone would've suspected. And yet his entire association with Jesus had been nothing but a charade.

Whispered Secrets

Judas was sweating bullets. Jesus knew; it was obvious. And yet the traitor kept up his charade a little while longer, trying to save face in front of the group. "Rabbi, is it I?" he asked (Matt. 26:25 NKJV). But his words gave him away. Translated in Greek, they indicate a presumed negative mixed with a fake innocence. It's like a suspicious mother walking into a room and her child immediately answering, "I didn't take the cookie"—with chocolate smeared on his face.

"Surely it is not I, Rabbi?" (NASB) one translation says. And Jesus simply replied, "You have said it" (Matt. 26:25 NKJV). Judas was caught with his hands in the cookie jar. Yet surprisingly, no one else picked up on this exchange. Either Jesus made the

comment quietly to Judas alone, or the other disciples, as always, were slow to catch on.

8. Judas had played his part well. No one would've ever suspected his role in the plot. But faced with Jesus at the table that night, Judas realized that his secret was out. He knew that Jesus saw what was in his heart. How did Jesus indicate to John who the traitor would be, according to John 13:26?

_____

_____

_____

Even that exchange must have taken place in whispered tones, because the other disciples *still* didn't realize that Christ was identifying Judas as the traitor. When He then told Judas, "What you do, do quickly" (John 13:27 NKJV), John says, "No one at the table knew for what reason He said this to him. For some thought, because Judas had the money box, that Jesus had said to him, 'Buy those things we need for the feast,' or that he should give something to the poor" (John 13:28–29 NKJV).

Mysteries aside, Jesus was tired of the charade game. It didn't matter whether the other disciples knew or not. He wanted to finish the Passover meal with His true friends, and so He sent Judas out. And for the traitor, these events in the Upper Room sealed his decision to betray Jesus that very night. He knew exactly how to do it because he knew Jesus' routine. Jesus would soon go to pray with His disciples at Gethsemane (John 18:2). And there, Judas could trap his teacher.

9. Why was it so hard for the disciples to understand Jesus' words and actions? What do you think were their thoughts when Judas got up and left the group?

_____

_____

_____

New Food

Jesus' last meal with His disciples wasn't just sort of important. It was the last Passover for all time. From that point on, the followers of Jesus celebrated the New Covenant ordinance known as the Lord's Supper. And so Jesus took some of the elements of the Passover meal and made them the elements of the Communion table.

First He took some of the unleavened bread and "blessed it"—or gave thanks to God for it. Then He broke it and distributed it to the disciples, saying, "Take, eat; this is My body." Imagine if you were one of the disciples sitting there. Pretty strange words, huh? Has Jesus gone nuts? Why is He talking about us eating His body? But it wasn't the first time Jesus had mentioned His body being consumed as life-giving

> For the life of the flesh is in the blood, and I have given it to you upon the altar to make atonement for your souls; for it is the blood that makes atonement for the soul.
>
> —Leviticus 17:11 NKJV

food. Earlier, He had described Himself as the bread of life, the true manna that had come from heaven (John 6).

After the bread was eaten, He took the cup of wine, again gave thanks, and said, "Drink from it, all of you. For this is My blood of the new covenant, which is shed for many for the remission of sins" (Matt. 26:27–28 NKJV). This would've most likely been the third of four cups of wine passed during a traditional Passover seder. Interestingly enough, this third cup was called "the cup of blessing," which is the same expression the apostle Paul uses to speak of the Communion cup in 1 Corinthians 10:16. Jesus blessed His followers with the symbol of His blood—a blessing we can never forget!

> Without shedding of blood there is no remission.
>
> —Hebrews 9:22 NKJV

DID YA KNOW?

The Greek verb for the giving of thanks is *eucharist*, from which we get Eucharist, the name often given to the observance of the Lord's Supper.

A New Covenant

The fact that Jesus called it "My blood of the new covenant" is significant. He wasn't just rattling off passing thoughts about a new order. His blood would establish a completely New Covenant. The Old Covenant involved spotless lambs being slaughtered. Remember all that blood flowing through Jerusalem during Passover? In the Hebrew culture, significant covenants were sealed by the shedding of blood. When someone entered into a solemn covenant with his neighbor, a sacrificial calf would be cut in two pieces and arranged on the ground. Then the parties in the covenant would walk together between the pieces of the slaughtered animal, signifying their willingness to be cut in pieces if they violated the covenant.

Sounds pretty gruesome, doesn't it? Yet it showed how serious Jews were about their promises. And as Christ passed the elements of this first Lord's Supper, it was no different.

10. Check out a couple of the covenants established with God in the Old Testament:

    How did God have Abraham prepare to seal their covenant in Genesis 15:9–18?

    _____

    _____

    _____

What did Moses do to include the Israelites in the Mosaic covenant in Exodus 24:5–8?

_____

_____

_____

11. The Jews were accustomed to sacrifice. At this time of year, the streets of Jerusalem literally ran with blood. It was necessary for the Old Covenant. Likewise, Jesus' blood was needed to seal the New Covenant. What do the following Scriptures have to say about the importance of blood?

Leviticus 17:11 —

_____

_____

_____

Hebrews 9:22 —

_____

_____

_____

> **Jesus' blood would establish a completely New Covenant.**

Some Christians treat Jesus' blood as if its molecules were supernatural. Remember, Jesus was fully human. His entire body was completely human, in every aspect. And so was His blood. The "power in the blood" that Christians talk about isn't in the actual fluid itself, but in the atonement He made for us.

An atonement is a reparation. It's a payment that satisfies a penalty or an offense. When you go to jail, you're required to pay bail money. Once that payment is made, your rights are restored. Our sin is an offense to God—so much that He can't have it in His presence. For our sin, we deserve more than a trip to the courthouse—we deserve death and separation from God (Rom. 6:23). But Christ's blood paid the price. His blood provided the atonement for our sin. That's why we honor His blood—not for some mysterious aura it had, but because of its sacrificial meaning that enables us to stand before God without being judged.

Here at the last Passover, Jesus passed the cup and said it symbolized blood shed for the remission of sins. The disciples would've understood this—but not how Jesus was meaning it. They knew the cup symbolized the death suffered by a sacrificial animal, and that a sacrificial lamb served as an atoning substitute for sinners.

But Christ had a deeper meaning. He wanted His disciples to understand what was happening when they saw Him bleeding and dying at the hands of Roman executioners. He wasn't a hapless victim of wicked men. He was sovereignly fulfilling His role as the Lamb of God—the great Passover Lamb—who takes away sin.

Obviously, the disciples couldn't have grasped the full meaning of Jesus' words that evening. Only after His death and resurrection did most of these truths become clear to them. They undoubtedly sensed that something momentous was occurring, but they would've been at a loss to explain it that evening.

As the meal ended, Matthew records that they sang a hymn—probably Psalm 118, the last hymn of the Hallel, which was the traditional way to end a Passover seder. They had just completed the last Passover meal. Either while still in the Upper Room or shortly after leaving, Jesus prayed the lengthy prayer recorded in John 17—His high priestly prayer. And then they left for the Mount of Olives. Only Jesus fully understood the awful events that lay ahead.

Wrapping It Up

The disciples prepared to go out into the Garden for a stroll in the cool of the night with their Master. Stretching their limbs, settling their supper, and spending some time in prayer—that's all they expected. All the activities of the feast day were winding down. None of them suspected that their long night of fear had just begun. They were on the threshold of a series of events that would bring about everything all the previous Passovers had foreshadowed. The true Lamb of God was about to be sacrificed for the sins of the world.

Things to Remember

- The blood flowing through the streets of Jerusalem was a graphic reminder of the awful price of sin.
- Jesus spent His last evening keeping the Passover with His closest friends.
- Taking the role of the lowest servant, Christ transformed the washing ceremony into an object lesson about humility and true holiness.
- Among this close-knit band of men who trusted one another like brothers, there was a betrayer.
- Jesus was about to fulfill His role as the Lamb of God—the great Passover Lamb—who takes away sin.

Memorize This!

Without shedding of blood there is no remission.
—Hebrews 9:22 NKJV

Check This Out

If you want to find out more about the following related topics, check out John MacArthur's extensive resources in the *MacArthur LifeWorks Library CD-ROM*, or visit www.gty.org.

✠ The Passover seder
✠ Washing the disciples' feet
✠ Jesus' servanthood
✠ Sacrificial atonement
✠ Covenants
✠ The New Covenant
✠ The Lord's Supper

Notes

Lesson 3

Your Will Be Done

✠

---

*"O My Father, if this cup cannot pass away from
Me unless I drink it, Your will be done."*
—Matthew 26:42 NKJV

The Word to the Wise

Before starting this lesson, read Matthew 26:36–44.

For Starters

Something was up. It was hard to put a finger on it, but each of the disciples had sensed the change in Jesus. Things had seemed a little tense through the Passover feast, especially when Judas left so suddenly. Sure, Jesus had put them all at ease at the end by leading them in a song or two and then asking everyone if they wanted to take a stroll in the Garden. But something was in the air, something ominous. Though they couldn't know what was coming, the disciples still felt Jesus' sadness. They had walked with Him for three years, yet they were at a loss for how to help Him now. And so they did the best they could: they stayed near Him during His last night.

The Clock Strikes 12:00

By the time Jesus reached Gethsemane with His disciples, it would've been nearing midnight. They were all tired. It was the end of a hectic week and the close of a busy day. Nothing sounded better than a nice, long snooze. But Christ had business in the Garden that was more important than sleep, and nothing would stop Him from going there to pray.

1. The disciples were used to seeing Jesus pray. He often went off by Himself to pray with His Father.

   Name three times that Jesus went off to pray alone.

   _____

   _____

   _____

> He Himself often withdrew into the wilderness and prayed.
>
> —Luke 5:16 NKJV

Name at least one time Jesus invited others to come and pray with Him.

_____

_____

_____

> It is a fearful thing to fall into the hands of the living God.
>
> —Hebrews 10:31 NKJV

2. On more than one occasion, Jesus' prayers resulted in miraculous answers. Perhaps that's why the disciples approached Him, saying, "Lord, teach us to pray" (Luke 11:1 NKJV). When Jesus prayed, things happened!

What happened when Jesus prayed in Luke 3:21?

_____

_____

_____

How about in Luke 9:29?

_____

_____

_____

———— ✠ ————

NO DOUBT

A lot of people doubt whether Jesus ever really existed, but there's plenty of proof to back it up, including some of the following historians who wrote about Him:

- Around AD 114, the Roman historian Tacitus wrote that the founder of the Christian religion, Jesus Christ, was put to death by Pontius Pilate in the reign of the Roman Emperor Tiberius (Annals 15.44).
- Pliny the Younger wrote a letter to the Emperor Trajan on the subject of Christ and Christians (Letters 10.96–97).
- In AD 90, the Jewish historian Josephus penned a short biographical note on Jesus: "Now there was about this time Jesus, a wise man, if it be lawful to call Him a man, for He was a doer of wonderful works, a teacher of such men as received the truth with pleasure . . . He was Christ" (Antiquities 18.63).
- Even the Talmud refers to Jesus of Nazareth (Sanhedrin 43a, Abodah Zerah 16b–17a).

Jesus isn't a myth. He came to earth and lived completely as a man. History proves it. —*Truth for Today*

We often think of Jesus as this divine being who floated through life on earth with His feet barely touching the ground. Even art throughout history has separated Jesus from the rest of us with a halo floating around His head. After all, He *was* God's son.

Though that's true, it's crucial to remember that Jesus gave up His position on the throne of heaven. When He came to earth, He became fully human in every sense. As a baby, He messed His diapers just like the rest of us did. As a kid, He had the same scrapes, bruises, and snotty noses that we all did. And as an adult, He was limited by the same emotions and physical symptoms. He got tired (John 4:6; Mark 4:38). He got hungry (Matt. 21:18). He got thirsty (John 4:7; 19:28). At times we see Jesus weeping and mourning (John 11:35; Luke 19:41). On a few occasions, He showed anger (John 2:15–17). And though Scripture never actually says that Christ laughed or smiled, it's kind of silly to assume He went through life with a gloomy look plastered on His face, isn't it? After all, we know He rejoiced, particularly when sinners were converted (Luke 15:4–32). His reputation among the Pharisees certainly suggests that He wasn't an unfriendly loner, but a joyful and gregarious "friend of tax collectors and sinners" (Luke 7:34 NKJV).

But it's easy to think of Jesus as filled with sorrow and grief. Why? Because that's the picture most of Scripture paints. Like a yearbook photo that doesn't capture your entire personality, the Bible's snapshot of Jesus leans mostly toward the sad side.

3. Why do you think the Bible portrays Jesus as more gloomy than joyful?

_____

_____

_____

4. Isaiah 53 is the familiar passage in which it was foretold that the coming Messiah would be a Man of sorrows. Fill in the blanks of Isaiah 53:3–4 here.

He is _____ and _____ by men, a Man of _____ and _____ with _____.

And we _____, as it were, our _____ from Him;

He was _____, and we did not _____ Him.

Surely He has _____ our _____ and

_____ our _____; yet we esteemed Him

_____, _____ by God, and _____ (NKJV).

Perhaps God's Word emphasizes Jesus' sorrow strictly for us. When you're going through a major time of grief, isn't it comforting to know that God Himself has been where you are? Most of us would prefer an understanding God to one who only

> When Jesus came to earth, He became fully human in every sense.

> "My soul is exceedingly sorrowful, even to death."
>
> —Matthew 26:38 NKJV

knows happiness and who can't relate when we're going through tough times. Because as we all know, life can be tough.

Jesus' pain was real, just as our pain is real. And there was no greater pain than what He began to bear that night in the Garden. As He spoke to His Father, every sorrow He'd ever known seemed to assault Him at once. That, combined with an obvious sense of dread for the ordeal He faced on the following day, gives us a remarkable insight into "the Man Christ Jesus."

DID YA KNOW?

Gethsemane was a garden planted with olive trees. The name comes from an Aramaic word meaning "olive press," suggesting that it was a place where olives were harvested and made into oil. In all likelihood it was a private garden owned by someone friendly to Christ who permitted Him to retreat there with His close disciples, in order to get away from the activity of city life for times of private prayer and instruction. There's still a thriving olive grove on that site today, with a few trees more than two thousand years old. Those same trees may well have been mute witnesses to the drama on that fateful evening.

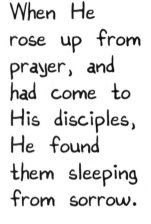

When He rose up from prayer, and had come to His disciples, He found them sleeping from sorrow.

—Luke 22:45 NKJV

A Reason for Sadness

The truth is, as bad as things get for us, we'll never know the misery Jesus had to endure starting that night. We could never comprehend the depth of Christ's agony because, frankly, we can't perceive the wickedness of sin as He could. Nor can we understand the terrors of divine wrath the way He did.

Can you imagine His thoughts? His own Father had designed this for Him. *This*—this horrible, public, humiliating path to death—was His life's goal. It was what He was designed for. And here in the midst of being burdened with the sin of the world, His Father couldn't help Him. In fact, after serving His Father faithfully every second of His life, Jesus was feeling His own Father's wrath.

TWO SIDES TO THE STORY

God's wrath is crucial to who He is. All His attributes are balanced in divine perfection. Sure, most of us think of Him as a loving God which He is, and then some. But He also hates sin big-time. And if He didn't have righteous anger to go along with His love, He wouldn't be God. Apart from His wrath, the concept of His love is meaningless. Furthermore, God hates sin just as perfectly and as thoroughly as He loves fallen sinners. One side without the other is utterly hollow.
—*Ashamed of the Gospel*

5. God can't be in the presence of sin. As the eternal judge, He can do nothing but condemn it and release His holy wrath. So when Jesus took on the sin of all mankind, He was placing Himself as the target of God's unimaginable wrath. What do the Scriptures tell us about the wrath of God? Match up these verses here.

___Jeremiah 10:10   a. God's wrath is revealed against ungodliness and unrighteousness.

___Ezekiel 22:31   b. At the wrath of God, the earth will tremble. None can endure it.

___Nahum 1:2   c. The wrath of God comes upon the sons of disobedience.

___Romans 1:18   d. God's indignation results in the consuming fire of His wrath.

___Ephesians 5:6   e. God is a jealous avenger, reserving wrath for His enemies.

"My food is to do the will of Him who sent Me, and to finish His work."

—John 4:34 NKJV

6. Hebrews 10:31 sums up one source of Jesus' sorrow. Fill in the blanks.

"It is a _____ thing to _____ into the _____ of the _____ _____" (NKJV).

Can you imagine how alone Jesus felt? It's likely that the disciples picked up on Jesus' sadness. But they didn't do a thing to help Him. According to Luke's account, they decided to drown their own sorrows with sleep (Luke 22:45). Jesus had asked them to do just one thing: stay awake. He wanted their support in this, the worst point of His life. He just needed their prayers. What did He get instead? Zzzzzz . . .

7. Jesus didn't try to hide His sadness from His friends. What did He tell them in Matthew 26:38?

_____

_____

_____

> "I do not seek My own will but the will of the Father who sent Me."
>
> —John 5:30 NKJV

Sleeping It Off

Gethsemane was probably a walled olive grove. It seems to have had a single entrance, and Jesus left most of the disciples at that entrance while He went inside to pray with Peter, James, and John. Why did He choose these three? They were part of Christ's "inner circle," His closest friends, from whom He needed intimate support right now.

The disciples left at the entrance of the Garden may have been accustomed to watching the gate in case anyone tried to disturb the Lord while He praying. John indicates the group had been there many times before. On this particular night, they should also have been engaged in prayer for themselves. According to Luke, Jesus instructed them all, "Pray that you may not enter into temptation" (Luke 22:40 NKJV). Matthew records that He awoke Peter, James, and John after they fell asleep the first and second times, and He repeated the admonition each time. Yet there's no suggestion that any of the disciples ever uttered a single word of prayer. Instead, they ignored their Master's words and chose the comfortable route by meeting their bodies' wants and drifting off to sleep.

How many times have we done the same thing? We pay more attention to our fleshly desires and remain oblivious to our own spiritual poverty and weakness—even when Christ has told us to keep watch! Despite being exhausted, despite surely wanting to drown His despair with sleep, despite wanting to give in to every easy answer, Jesus refused to take the convenient path. He couldn't sleep when the need to commune with His Father was so great. He needed strength.

> Jesus refused to take the convenient path. He couldn't sleep when the need to commune with His Father was so great. He needed strength.

8. Jesus reached out to God at His weakest moment. What does 2 Corinthians 12:9–10 say about God's strength when we are weak?

_____

_____

_____

How could the disciples fall asleep? Before you start pointing the finger of blame, think about this: Christ's words (whether of warning or insight) often went over their heads. Remember, He'd talked about His coming death a few times before, and each episode had led to confused looks and befuddled stares. So when Jesus talked about His broken body and spilled blood that night at dinner, what made them think anything was out of the ordinary? He'd always spoken in code (at least for them).

Granted, Luke 22:45 allows us to give the disciples some credit. They knew Jesus was in pain. Their own sorrow for Him drove them to sleep. When you're depressed and confused, wouldn't you rather sleep than deal with the problem? Likewise, the disciples' troubled minds were seeking an escape. And so they fell asleep, leaving Jesus to bear His anguish all alone.

Sweating Blood

Jesus wasn't exaggerating when He told the disciples that His distress was so severe that it had brought Him to the very brink of death. The agony He bore in the Garden was literally enough to kill Him—and probably would've done so if God weren't preserving Him for another means of death. Luke records that "His sweat became like great drops of blood falling down to the ground" (Luke 22:44 NKJV).

Here's where things begin to get crazy. Luke's description isn't an exaggeration just to make this story more dramatic. Jesus' sweating blood is a rare but well-documented malady known as *hematidrosis* that sometimes occurs under heavy emotional distress. Capillaries directly beneath the skin burst under stress, and the blood mixes with a person's perspiration, exiting through the sweat glands.

"I always do those things that please Him."

—John 8:29 NKJV

Why was Jesus feeling such agony? It's natural to assume He was dreading the physical pain of the cross and the tortures He would suffer on the way to Calvary. But in truth, tons of people have suffered crucifixion without sweating blood at the thought of it. It's hard to believe that the Son of God would be wracked with such incredible agony over the fear of what men could do to Him. After all, Jesus was as fearless as they come. He'd once taught: "Do not fear those who kill the body but cannot kill the soul" (Matt. 10:28 NKJV). Jesus knew what was going on.

He also wasn't scared of death. He had come to die. Was Jesus having second thoughts about dying? John 12:27 records an earlier prayer of Jesus, spoken in public, in which He said, "Now My soul is troubled, and what shall I say? 'Father, save Me from this hour'? But for this purpose I came to this hour" (NKJV).

Nope. Again, Jesus knew the situation.

Let This Cup Pass

So what was it that led to these initial drops of blood? Why such despair?

As Jesus was crying out to His father in the Garden, He prays, "O My Father, if it is possible, let this cup pass from Me." Later, when Jesus is being arrested and Peter tries to use his sword to stop the arrest, "Jesus said to Peter, 'Put your sword into the sheath. Shall I not drink the cup which My Father has given Me?'" (John 18:11 NKJV). So there's something about the *cup* that Jesus is concerned about.

What is the cup? It's not merely death. It isn't the physical pain of the cross. It wasn't the scourging or the humiliation. It wasn't the horrible thirst, the torture of having nails driven through His body, or the disgrace of being spat upon or beaten. It wasn't even all those things combined. All of those were the very things Christ Himself had said not to fear. He said, "And I say to you, My friends, do not be afraid of those who kill the body, and after that have no more that they can do" (Luke 12:4 NKJV).

"But," He went on to add, "I will show you whom you should fear: Fear Him who, after He has killed, has power to cast into hell; yes, I say to you, fear Him!" (v. 5 NKJV). Clearly, what Christ dreaded most about the cross—the cup from which He asks to be delivered if possible—was the outpouring of divine wrath He would have to endure from His holy Father.

9. Similar imagery using a cup to symbolize divine judgment is found throughout the Old Testament. Match up these examples.

___	Isaiah 51:17	a.	Edom, the cup shall also pass over to you.
___	Jeremiah 25:15–16	b.	I will put the cup of horror and desolation in your hands.
___	Lamentations 4:21–22	c.	Take this wine cup of fury from My hand.
___	Ezekiel 23:31–34	d.	Awake, you who have drunk the cup of His fury.
___	Habakkuk 2:16	e.	The cup of the Lord's right hand will turn against you.

> The cup was a well-known Old Testament symbol of divine wrath against sin.

The cup was a well-known Old Testament symbol of divine wrath against sin. So when Christ prayed that, if possible, the cup might pass from Him, He spoke of drinking the cup of divine judgment. Forget any notions you have that Christ feared the earthly pain of crucifixion. If He was truly the Son of God, He wouldn't have even blinked at the thought of what men could do to Him.

What sent Christ into such misery was sin. Yours. Mine. All of ours . . . for all of time. Talk about an overwhelming weight. Jesus knew that the next day He would "bear the sins of many" (Heb. 9:28 NKJV), and the fullness of divine wrath would fall on Him. In some mysterious way that our human minds could never fathom, God the Father would turn His face from Christ the Son, and Christ would bear the full brunt of the divine fury against sin.

A Divine Pleasure

So you think that's crazy, huh? Then check this out. Isaiah 53:10 says, "It pleased the Lord to bruise Him; He has put Him to grief" (NKJV).

What?!? How in the world could it *please* God to see His own Son suffer His terrible wrath?

The answer is the same reason Christ ultimately chose to go through with this divine yet horrific plan. It's the same reason He said yes to more than forty-eight hours of literal hell on earth. And it's essentially the reason He came in the first place.

You. Me. All of us . . . for all time.

When Christ hung on the cross, He was bearing the sins of us all and He was suffering the wrath of God on our behalf. Second Corinthians 5:21 explains the cross in a similar way: "He made Him who knew no sin to be sin for us" (NKJV). In other words, on the cross, God assigned our sin to Christ and then punished Him for it.

> The world is passing away, and the lust of it; but he who does the will of God abides forever.
>
> —1 John 2:17 NKJV

10. Most of us have heard John 3:16 quoted our whole lives. Think about it now in light of Jesus' suffering. Write out a new "version" of this verse, recalling the horrible death God the Father and the Son knew about yet overlooked in order to save us.

_____

_____

_____

Sin costs something. It has a price. When we disobey our parents, we're grounded. When we break a rule in school, we get detention (or worse). When we break a law, we end up paying money or time (or both). These are all simply extrapolations from God's ultimate law of sin, which says that when we sin, a repercussion is in order. Disease. Famine. Bombings. Hijackings. These all result from sin. And it's no coincidence the earth is full of these things, simply because we live in a fallen, sinful world.

To offer a way out of this madness, a price had to be paid for sin. But it wasn't just a fee to pay off sin for a few hours, a couple days, or even an entire year. Jesus anted up for all of time. He was the only one able to pay such a price.

And He paid it in full—which explains His cry of anguish in Matthew 27:46: "My God, My God, why have You forsaken Me?" (NKJV). That cry from the cross reflected the extreme bitterness of the cup He was given. No wonder He wanted to pass on the cup assigned to Him.

But if Jesus knew full well that He was the only one who could pay the price for humanity's sin, why did He ask for the cup to pass from Him? Because this was an honest expression of the dread He was feeling at the moment. He wasn't crossing His fingers, hoping someone else could sub in for Him as chief sin-bearer. In fact, that's made clear by the remainder of His prayer: "Nevertheless, not as I will, but as You will" (Matt. 26:39 NKJV). Notice that the second time He prayed, "O My Father, if this cup cannot pass away from Me unless I drink it, Your will be done" (26:42). As the intensity of the agony increased, so did the sense of Jesus' determination to do the will of His Father.

Committed & Submitted

Remember once more that Jesus was completely human. He wasn't just playing at being human. He didn't have a God suit underneath His skin that protected Him from _real_ human feelings, emotions, and reactions. And at this moment in the Garden, His humanity manifested itself as clearly as ever during His ministry.

But just as powerfully manifested was Jesus' unbelievable commitment to do His Father's will. He was completely submitted. His prayer at Gethsemane underscores His devotion to His Father. But it also reflects the honest expression of His human feelings. He sincerely dreaded the prospect of the Father's wrath, and He wished to avoid it if there had been any possible way.

When Christ hung on the cross, He was bearing the sins of us all and He was suffering the wrath of God on our behalf.

11. Jesus voluntarily submitted to His Father's will. How do the following verses define Jesus' personal purpose on earth?

John 5:30 —

_____

_____

_____

John 6:38 —

_____

_____

_____

John 8:29 —

_____

_____

_____

Jesus' prayer is a moment-by-moment tutorial in how to line up with God's will.

Christ's prayer was above all a prayer of submission. The real gist of the prayer wasn't the request to let the cup pass but the still higher purpose reflected in His repeated request, "Your will be done" (Matt. 26:42 NKJV). Each wave of His praying stressed the same thing: "My Father, if it is possible, let this cup pass from Me; nevertheless, *not as I will, but as You will*" (Matt. 26:39 NKJV). "O My Father, if this cup cannot pass away from Me unless I drink it, *Your will be done*" (Matt. 26:42 NKJV). "He left them, went away again, and prayed the third time, *saying the same words*" (Matt. 26:44 NKJV; *emphasis added* in all preceding quotations).

As any of us would've had, Jesus' natural human desire was to avoid, if possible, the awful judgment He was about to suffer. But His overriding desire—the ultimate answer to prayer He was pleading for—was that God's will be done.

12. According to 1 John 2:17, what happens when you do God's will?

_____

_____

_____

There's a huge lesson for us to learn here. Jesus' prayer is a moment-by-moment tutorial in how to line up with God's will. His natural, *human* emotions didn't want to submit to God's plan. But through prayer, through surrendering His will to the will of the Father, He remained perfectly obedient to God.

But there's a deeper lesson. Remember that Christ had no sinful appetites, no desires that were perverted by sin, no inclination ever to do wrong. If *He* needed to submit His appetites and passions to the will of God with such deliberate, purposeful dedication, then how much more do we need to be deliberate in surrendering our hearts, our souls, our minds, and our strength to God? If we want to have any chance of glorifying and pleasing God with our lives, we have to consciously submit *every part* of our lives to the will of God.

Wrapping It Up

When Christ finished praying, He got what He was ultimately looking for: He emerged from His agony in perfect harmony with the will of His Father. He was prepared to face the Cross and drink the bitter cup of the Father's wrath against sin. His enemies were already approaching. The calmness with which Christ would meet them—and the quiet grace He would show throughout His whole ordeal—are graphic proof that God the Father heard and answered His Son's heart's cry in Gethsemane.

Things to Remember

- Christ had business in the Garden that was more important than sleep, and nothing would stop Him from going there to pray.
- During Jesus' prayer that night in the Garden, every sorrow He'd ever known seemed to assault Him at once.
- From Jesus' example, the disciples would learn a great lesson in how to handle affliction.
- What Christ dreaded most about the Cross was the divine wrath He'd have to endure from His holy Father.
- It *pleased* both the Father and the Son to endure this horrible time in order to pay the price for all of us, for all time.
- As the intensity of the agony increased, so did the sense of Jesus' determination to do His Father's will.
- If we want to have any chance of glorifying and pleasing God with our lives, we have to consciously submit *every part* of our lives to the will of God.

Memorize This!

The world is passing away, and the lust of it; but he who does the will of God abides forever.
—1 John 2:17 NKJV

If we want to have any chance of glorifying and pleasing God with our lives, we have to consciously submit *every part* of our lives to the will of God.

Check This Out

If you want to find out more about the following related topics, check out John MacArthur's extensive resources in the *MacArthur LifeWorks Library CD-ROM*, or visit www.gty.org.

✠ Doing God's will
✠ Submission
✠ Sorrow and affliction
✠ The priority of prayer
✠ The wrath of God against sin
✠ The price of redemption

Lesson 4

Stabbed in the Back

✠

"Judas, are you betraying the Son of Man with a kiss?"
—Luke 22:48 NKJV

The Word to the Wise

Before starting this lesson, read Matthew 26:45–56.

For Starters

The grove at Gethsemane was their favorite spot. It had become their secret haven from the many followers and admirers of Jesus. Sheltered by overhanging boughs of olive trees, they could rest from the pressing crowds or gather to pray. The Garden was just far enough from the city's noise to be peaceful, familiar, soothing, and safe. But on this night, the disciples learned with a jolt that their secret had been betrayed. Their haven was under attack. And one of their own was found leading the enemy right into their midst.

Sure Defeat

From a human vantage point, the remaining events of this tragic Passover night seem to bring nothing but disgrace and defeat for the Son of God. It's easy to think that Jesus' prayer in the Garden fell on deaf ears, that His Father didn't respond, and that everything from that point on suddenly spun out of control for Jesus.

Most likely, that's exactly what the disciples thought too. They had never been in a situation like this before. Sure, Jesus had been challenged by hostile Pharisees and Sadducees before, but He'd always confounded and silenced them. On several occasions, His enemies tried to take Him by force or threatened Him with bodily harm. But He'd always slipped through their fingers, sometimes by miraculous means.

The disciples were used to seeing Jesus win. He was God's Son, after all, so why wouldn't He always be victorious in conflict or pursuit? For the three (Peter, James, and John) who were physically closest to Him that night, they may have heard requests to the Father in between their snores. Surely God would answer His prayers, right?

> "Do you think that I cannot now pray to My Father, and He will provide Me with more than twelve legions of angels?"
>
> —Matthew 26:53 NKJV

1. Sometimes it seems our prayers aren't heard, as if we have to get God's attention. We're not alone. Take a look at these passages from the Old Testament and match them up.

___ 2 Chronicles 6:35   a. Hear my just cause; attend to my cry.

___ Nehemiah 1:6   b. Bow down your ear, O LORD, hear me.

___ Psalm 17:1   c. God's ears are attentive and His eyes open to prayer.

___ Psalm 39:12   d. Hear my prayer, and in Your faithfulness answer me.

___ Psalm 86:1   e. Hear our prayers and supplications; maintain our cause.

___ Psalm 143:1   f. Do not be silent at my tears.

2. The truth is, God *always* hears our prayers (Scripture says so repeatedly). In fact, He often anticipates our pleas. How does Isaiah 65:24 describe God's response to our call?

_____

_____

_____

> The disciples were used to seeing Jesus win. He was God's Son, after all, so why wouldn't He always be victorious in conflict or pursuit? The disciples were used to seeing Jesus win. He was God's Son, after all, so why wouldn't He always be victorious in conflict or pursuit?

Suddenly everything began to go wrong—or so it seemed. An armed mob arrived on the scene to arrest Jesus. Judas quite unexpectedly betrayed Him in the most despicable manner: with a hypocritical kiss. When Peter tried to intervene with force, Jesus stopped him with a stern rebuke. Finally, the disciples, gripped with fear, abandoned their Master and fled. Each turn of events seemed to bring more disgrace and defeat upon Jesus. For anyone watching the scene that night, it seemed like the end of the world.

And yet amid the chaos of the scene, Jesus' calm, triumphant demeanor remained uncompromised throughout. Every biblical account paints the picture of Christ standing in complete control while the world around Him appeared to collapse.

———— ✠ ————

DID YA KNOW?

Even at this late stage of the game, Matthew still refers to Judas as "one of the twelve" (Matt. 26:47 NKJV). He's often designated that way in the New Testament. In fact, all four Gospels use the expression to describe Judas (Mark 14:10, 43; Luke 22:47; John 6:71). The Gospel writers deliberately stressed Judas's status as one of the Twelve to accent the sense of shock and betrayal they all felt when he turned out to be a traitor.

———— ✠ ————

The Real Battle

Mel Gibson's movie, *The Passion of the Christ*, artistically depicted the scene at the Garden of Gethsemane as an intense spiritual battle between Jesus and the ultimate tempter, Satan. While Christ prayed for His Father's will, Satan lurked with his list of "easy outs." *You don't have to go through with this. Is this really necessary? After all, You're the Son of God. Has Your Father abandoned You?*

It was all too familiar. Satan had tempted Christ at the beginning of His ministry, and Christ had withstood every one of his ploys (Matt. 4:1–11)—and never let up all through His life. But the agony in the Garden represents a final, desperate frontal assault from the Evil One, and Christ had again emerged victorious. Earlier, Christ had told His disciples that Satan "has nothing in Me" (John 14:30 NKJV). There truly was nothing in Him that Satan could take advantage of.

3. As Christians, our enemy isn't made up of flesh and blood. In Ephesians 6:12, what does Paul say we struggle with?

_____

_____

_____

> "Lord, I am ready to go with You, both to prison and to death."
>
> —Luke 22:33 NKJV

4. Jesus remained outwardly calm because the true battle was spiritual. What else do the Scriptures tell us about these principalities? What does Paul tell us in Colossians 1:16 about the principalities and powers?

_____

_____

_____

According to Romans 8:38–39, what can those principalities do to God's relationship with us?

_____

_____

_____

What did Jesus eventually do to the principalities and powers that tried to do battle against Him, according to Colossians 2:15?

_____

_____

_____

Mob Overkill

Judas seemed like such a regular guy. He hadn't done anything to tip off the disciples as to his plan to betray Jesus. In fact, he'd always gone far to the other extreme, making sure everyone thought of him as the guy whom Jesus trusted enough to put in charge of the group's money. But Judas's facade of faithfulness to Christ makes his treachery that much more despicable. Christ being handed over by a sworn enemy would've been understandable . . . but a close friend?

To make matters worse, Judas brought a large mob armed with swords and clubs. They were prepared for violence. They were set to do bodily harm to Christ and the disciples, if necessary. And this wasn't just an impromptu mob of citizens; this was a hand-selected band of thugs, carefully organized by the chief priests and elders.

Luke says the mob included members of the temple guard ("captains of the temple"—Luke 22:52 NKJV). These were security officers who acted as policemen in the temple grounds and had limited powers (sanctioned by Rome) to arrest people for violations of the Jewish law (John 7:32).

John notes that the mob also included a detachment of Roman soldiers (John 18:3). Since the arrest of Jesus had been orchestrated by the Sanhedrin, they must have been the ones who requested the soldiers to participate in taking Jesus. Obviously they planned to try Him on capital charges, and since only Rome had authority to carry out the death penalty, it was necessary to have a contingent of soldiers involved at the time of the arrest. To gain the army's support in capturing Jesus, the chief priests had probably told the Roman authorities that Jesus was an anti-Roman insurrectionist.

None of the Gospels says how large the mob was, but Matthew, Mark, and Luke all agree that it was a multitude (Mark 14:43; Luke 22:47). The crowd could've easily numbered in the hundreds. Why would such a huge number of tactically trained warriors be sent to deal with twelve commoners and a notorious pacifist? Two words: Jesus' power. The chief priests were clearly frightened of this mysterious Jesus with supernatural power. His past miracles likely caused them to assume He would rely on some kind of magic and sorcery to resist arrest.

Jesus Himself called attention to their absurd and cowardly tactic of sending an armed multitude to arrest Him in the middle of the night. "Have you come out, as against a robber, with swords and clubs to take Me? I sat daily with you, teaching in the temple, and you did not seize Me" (Matt. 26:55 NKJV). Such a large group was clearly overkill.

It was also pointless. Jesus wasn't about to resist. Of course, if He hadn't been *willing* to be arrested, no amount of earthly force would've been sufficient to capture Him.

5. If Jesus had wanted to, He could've easily escaped even from such a large mob. What did He point out to Peter in Matthew 26:53?

_____

_____

_____

> "Lord, why can I not follow You now? I will lay down my life for Your sake."
>
> —John 13:37 NKJV

DID YA KNOW?

In His rebuke of Peter, Jesus said, "Do you think that I cannot now pray to My Father, and He will provide Me with more than twelve legions of angels?" (Matt. 26:53 NKJV). A legion was comprised of 6,000 soldiers. Twelve angelic legions would be 72,000 angels. Bear in mind that in the Old Testament—when Sennacherib's armies threatened Jerusalem—a single angel slew 185,000 Assyrian troops *in one night* (2 Kings 19:35). So the military might of 72,000 angels would be pretty intimidating, to say the least! If Christ had intended to be rescued from this armed mob, He definitely wouldn't have needed Peter's help.

Sealed with a Kiss

It would've been very dark in Gethsemane at that hour. Passover always fell on a full moon, so it was brighter than most nights; but in an olive grove the moonlight would barely provide enough light to make dim shadows in the darkness. So Judas had previously arranged a signal to let his fellow conspirators know which one was Jesus.

It's also possible that Judas intended the disciples to have a Plan B up their sleeves. Another disciple could've easily surrendered to the authorities in Jesus' place, pretending to be Him in order to spare His life. After all, just hours before in the Upper Room, Judas had listened while each of the other disciples had professed his willingness to go to prison or die for Christ.

6. According to Luke 22:33, what two things had the disciples promised Jesus?

_____

_____

_____

> You ought to be quiet and do nothing rashly.
>
> —Acts 19:36 NKJV

Judas had told the soldiers, "Whomever I kiss, He is the One; seize Him" (Matt. 26:48 NKJV). In that culture, a kiss was a sign of respect and homage as well as affection. Slaves kissed the feet of their masters as the utmost sign of respect. Disciples sometimes kissed the hem of their teacher's garment as a token of reverence and deep devotion. It was common to kiss someone on the hand as a gesture of respect and honor. But a kiss on the face, especially with an embrace, signified personal friendship and affection. The gesture was reserved for the closest of friends, so that a disciple wouldn't ordinarily embrace and kiss his teacher unless the teacher first offered the kiss.

As if it weren't enough for Judas to betray Jesus, the traitor topped it off by pretending to share the utmost affection for His teacher. Apparently, Judas had no shame whatsoever. He could've chosen any signal for identifying Christ to his fellow conspirators. But he deliberately chose one that capped his own guilt with the most extreme hypocrisy.

> So they said, "Lord, look, here are two swords." And He said to them; "It is enough."
>
> —Luke 22:38 NKJV

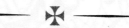

DID YA KNOW?

The word Matthew employs to describe Judas's kiss is *kataphileo*, which means, "to kiss earnestly, intensively, or repeatedly." It's the same word used to describe the affectionate worship lavished on Jesus by the woman at the Pharisee's house who anointed His feet with fragrant oil, wiped them with her hair, and repeatedly kissed [*kataphileo*] them (Luke 7:38).

"But Jesus said to him, 'Friend, why have you come?'" (Matt. 26:50 NKJV). Jesus' question seems strange to some. Didn't He know full well why His traitor was here? Of course He did. His point was to allow Judas to face up to—and the other disciples to recognize—what an evil thing he was doing. But Judas didn't break stride. With bold-faced treachery, he handed Jesus over to His executioners, still pretending affection yet nurturing the most deep-seated hatred in his heart.

SO WHAT HAPPENED TO JUDAS?

Surely the bad guy in this story got what was coming to him, didn't he? Oh boy, did he ever. Matthew is the only Gospel that includes the last part of Judas's story (Matt. 27:3–10). Basically, this traitor immediately recognized the huge mistake he'd made. He took his blood money back to the priests and threw it in their faces. Then he went and hanged himself. But Acts 1:18 takes it a step further, detailing how he *really* died. Apparently, Judas chose to hang himself on a tree growing above some jagged rocks. Either the rope or the tree branch broke, and Judas fell headfirst onto the rocks. The biblical description is graphic and ugly: "He burst open in the middle and all his entrails gushed out" (Acts 1:18 NKJV). Judas was so tragic that he couldn't even kill himself the way he wanted to.
—*Twelve Ordinary Men*

Preparing for Battle

The disciples may not have been mentally prepared for this attack. After all, the mob apparently came moments after Jesus awoke them from their sleep. But having heard all their teacher's talk of betrayal and His predictions about His arrest and Crucifixion, the disciples didn't go into the Garden unarmed.

7. What did Jesus tell the disciples earlier about swords, according to Luke 22:35–38?

_____

_____

_____

It seems somewhat strange for Christ to okay His disciples' carrying two swords into the Garden, only to later rebuke one of them for drawing his weapon. What gives?

Just as had been in His questioning of Judas, here Christ was presenting a figurative double-edged sword. It seemed as if He was preparing them for physical violence. But Jesus, as always, was more concerned about the spiritual realm. His words prior to entering Gethsemane were to prepare His disciples for the events of that night, so that their faith wouldn't be shaken. He was warning them of a spiritual battle they were about to face; He certainly wasn't telling them to arm themselves with fleshly weapons (2 Cor. 10:4). But the disciples mistakenly assumed that He literally meant for them to go and purchase swords. So they had taken a private inventory and found that they already had two swords among them. Jesus' ambiguous reply ("It is enough") probably meant "enough of such talk." They may have thought He meant two swords were sufficient. In any case, His remark served its purpose and they thought no more about arming themselves further.

The reality is, two measly swords would be practically useless against an armed mob that included so many Roman soldiers. Still, they were emboldened by something only John reports. When the attackers announced that they were seeking Jesus of Nazareth, "Jesus said to them, 'I am He.'. . . Now when He said to them, 'I am He,' they drew back and fell to the ground" (John 18:5–6 NKJV). For a brief moment, Jesus unveiled the full glory of His name—I AM. Just the mention of this sent people falling on their faces. This display of supernatural power probably got the disciples thinking, *Finally, Jesus is ready to unleash His miraculous power on these guys. Let's get in on this!* And so they asked Him if they should use their weapons.

Everyone, that is, except Peter. He apparently saw no point in thinking or talking at this point. John tells us, "Simon Peter, having a sword, drew it and struck the high priest's servant, and cut off his right ear. The servant's name was Malchus" (John 18:10 NKJV).

> "My kingdom is not of this world. If My kingdom were of this world, My servants would fight."
>
> —John 18:36 NKJV

DID YA KNOW?

Only John identifies Peter as the swordsman. It may be because the synoptic Gospels (Matthew, Mark, and Luke) were written much earlier, before Rome sacked Jerusalem and destroyed the temple. The Gospel writers may have refrained from identifying Peter because of the potential of reprisal from the Jewish leaders.

> "Shall I not drink the cup which My Father has given Me?"
>
> —John 18:11 NKJV

8. Jesus never intended for His disciples to take up weapons in His defense. How did He explain this to Pilate in John 18:36?

_____

_____

_____

WHAT WERE YOU THINKING?!?

There was nothing unusual about Galilean fishermen carrying swords. These were long double-edged knives or daggers rather than full-length fighting swords. They were carried in a leather sheath strapped to the belt, and they had several practical uses other than violence against other people. But think about it. There was an entire detachment of Roman soldiers there, perhaps numbering in the hundreds. What did Peter think he was going to do? Behead them all, one by one? Whatever his plans were, he took a swing at Malchus. He was undoubtedly trying to cut the man's head off, but only got his ear. After all, Peter was a fisherman, not a swordsman. —*The Murder of Jesus* and *Twelve Ordinary Men*

History is full of misguided Christians who have tried to advance the kingdom of God with force. From the Crusades to British slavery, people have offered Jesus or a knife to the throat. Such hypocrisy has undoubtedly hurt the cause of Christ more than it's helped it. But Christ's response to Peter's actions indicated the true heart of God. He quickly reminded His hot-blooded disciple that there was a higher purpose behind that night's chaos.

9. Peter's rash intervention couldn't have helped God's plan. In fact, by acting out of the flesh, Christ's own disciple became an obstacle—his actions could have sparked an entire massacre.

   What does James 1:20 tell us about acting out of anger?

   _____

   _____

   _____

   According to 2 Corinthians 10:4, what can our weapons *not* be?

   _____

   _____

   _____

Blinded Eyes & Reattached Ears

Malchus's severed ear was apparently still dangling from the side of his head. Obviously, it wasn't a pretty sight. In a remarkable display of Jesus' power, "He touched his ear and healed him" (Luke 22:51 NKJV). It's interesting to note that this is the only incident recorded in Scripture where Christ healed a fresh wound. Even more astounding is the fact that Malchus was an unbeliever, hostile to Christ. He was obviously out to get Jesus, yet the Son of God reacted with nothing but compassion.

But perhaps the most unbelievable part of this scene is that the miracle goes virtually ignored by the mob. They carried on with their evil business as if nothing out of the ordinary had happened (Luke 22:54). Wait a second: A guy just reattached a severed ear with nothing but his bare hands, and no one takes notice?

It's sad, but true. The healing of Malchus's ear had no more effect on their hearts than the powerful force that had knocked them to the ground a few moments before. Within a matter of minutes they had twice encountered the supernatural power of God, yet their eyes and hearts were blind to the truth. Even a miraculous display that proved Christ's deity wouldn't stop them from the evil goal they had set their hearts on.

> The wrath of man does not produce the righteousness of God.
>
> —James 1:20 NKJV

Running for Their Lives

> "Indeed the hour is coming, yes, has now come, that you will be scattered, each to his own."
>
> —John 16:32 NKJV

The disciples had repeatedly heard Jesus express absolute confidence in the sovereign plan of God. But at this moment, under these circumstances, it probably brought as much comfort to them as a Roman soldier's smile. They had just watched Christ betrayed into the hands of His enemies . . . and there was nothing they could do to stop it. Ever since they'd hung around Jesus, things had always worked out, no matter how hopeless a situation was. This certainly seemed as bad as it could get.

Remember, the disciples were already feeling low. They had chosen to sleep in the Garden rather than face their sorrow. Now utter despair was setting in. Their eyes were fixed firmly on the circumstances of the moment, not on the doctrine of God's sovereignty. And because of that, they couldn't draw comfort from Jesus' reassuring words. Fear overwhelmed them. "Then all the disciples forsook Him and fled" (Matt. 26:56 NKJV).

They ran like scared cats. Not that you or I would've done anything different . . . because even their desertion occurred so that the Scriptures might be fulfilled. They were acting precisely as Jesus said they would. Looking back on these events, they must have realized that not one disaster had happened that He hadn't previously warned them about.

The disciples literally scattered, rather than fleeing as a group. Peter and John secretly followed the mob to the high priest's house (John 18:15). Nothing is said about where the other disciples went—but they apparently went into hiding.

In fairness to them, the truth is that they all would've been arrested or worse if they had stayed in the Garden. That fact is evident from Jesus' plea to the arresting officers, recorded in John's account: "If you seek Me, let these go their way" (John 18:8 NKJV). According to John, Jesus said that "[So] that the saying might be fulfilled which He spoke, 'Of those whom You gave Me I have lost none'" (John 18:9 NKJV). It's likely that when they heard Jesus say those words, they seized the moment and ran like crazy.

10. Even though Jesus was abandoned by His disciples, was He utterly alone? What does John 16:32 say?

_____

_____

_____

MARK'S CAMEO

Mark includes a vignette found in none of the other Gospels: "They all forsook Him and fled. Now a certain young man followed Him, having a linen cloth thrown around his naked body. And the young men laid hold of him, and he left the linen cloth and fled from them naked" (14:50–52 NKJV). Who that "certain young man" was is nowhere stated, but it was probably Mark himself. The "young men" who laid hold of him were no doubt the Roman soldiers. Whoever this unnamed young man was, he had apparently been in bed, or preparing for bed, when the noise of the mob awakened him. Without taking time to dress, he threw on a linen cloth, perhaps a bed sheet (not *that* strange in those days), and followed the noise to see what was up. Assuming that he was a follower of Christ, the soldiers tried to apprehend him. He escaped, but only by abandoning his makeshift clothing and fleeing into the night naked.

> "If you seek Me, let these go their way."
>
> —John 18:8 NKJV

Wrapping It Up

They came against Him—a traitor leading the enemy's army. Under the cover of darkness, without a shred of evidence, and prepared for violence. The secret conspiracy of the religious rulers to destroy Jesus had cornered the Man and scattered His followers. But Jesus' response is a constant theme of all four Gospel accounts of the Crucifixion: "But all this was done that the Scriptures of the prophets might be fulfilled" (Matt. 26:56 NKJV). Despite their hostility to Christ, the men who arrested Him were fulfilling His sovereign purposes perfectly. Their attempts to destroy Him were only achieving His chosen ends, fulfilling a plan that was established before time began.

Things to Remember

- Judas's facade of faithfulness to Christ makes his treachery even more despicable.
- If Jesus hadn't been willing to be arrested, no amount of earthly force would've been sufficient to capture Him.
- Jesus healed the ear of an enemy out to get Him, showing His ever-present compassion for all.
- The disciples' eyes were fixed firmly on the circumstances of the moment.

Memorize This!

*Indeed the hour is coming, yes, has now come, that you will
be scattered, each to his own, and will leave Me alone. And
yet I am not alone, because the Father is with Me.*

—John 16:32 NKJV

Check This Out

If you want to find out more about the following related topics, check out John MacArthur's extensive resources in the *MacArthur LifeWorks Library CD-ROM*, or visit www.gty.org.

✠ Judas's betrayal
✠ Legions of angels
✠ Deceptions of the enemy
✠ Spiritual warfare
✠ Trusting God's sovereignty in the midst of a crisis

Lesson 5

Breaking Up

✠

It is written: "I will strike the Shepherd, and the sheep of the flock will be scattered."
—Matthew 26:31 NKJV

The Word to the Wise

Before starting this lesson, read Matthew 26:31–35.

For Starters

For three and a half years, Jesus had hung out with his closest friends. They had done everything together—traveling, eating, praying, laughing, talking. Christ had poured His life into this tight-knit group, teaching them all about the kingdom of God and how much the Father adored them. Though reluctant at first, the group came to believe in who Jesus was and pledged themselves to stay by His side through thick and thin. They just knew they'd be together to the bitter end.

Obviously, that didn't happen. Caught off-guard by the ambush of the enemy, all of Jesus' friends deserted Him in His hour of need. In their panic, they scattered like frightened sheep.

Big Words, Little Actions

Admit it. As a believer, you've probably thought through the situation in your head: You're staring down the barrel of a gun, and the person holding the weapon is forcing you to decide between denying your faith or dying on the spot. Say that you don't believe in Jesus and you live; confess that He's the way, the truth, and the life, and you're history.

Most of us would hope that we'd remain true to our Savior, just as He was true to us throughout His worst hours. We'd like to think that we would have the courage to stare death in the face and testify to God's faithfulness. And thank goodness, most of us have not, nor will not, ever face such a situation.

But there's a sad reality behind this thought. While most of us have never been in such extreme life-or-faith situations, we've encountered less-than-life-threatening situations and still denied Jesus. In the classroom. In the school hallway. At practice after school. Things have been said that directly attack God, and we've kept silent. Doors of spiritual searching from classmates have been opened, yet our mouths

> Strike the Shepherd, and the sheep will be scattered.
>
> —Zechariah 13:7 NKJV

> Most of us would hope that we'd remain true to our Savior, just as He was true to us throughout His worst hours.

remained shut. We tolerate unrighteousness when we ought to stand against it. We're timid when we ought to be bold. We do nothing when we ought to act.

Here's the truth: left to ourselves, apart from divine grace, we all lack the strength and fortitude to stand up for Christ in the face of hostility.

> "Those whom You gave Me I have kept; and none of them is lost except the son of perdition."
>
> —John 17:12 NKJV

1. Throughout the Bible, men and women prayed for the boldness to do and say the right thing. Here are just a few examples of this—match them up.

    ___ Psalm 138:3   a. Grant us boldness to speak Your Word.
    ___ Proverbs 28:1   b. Pray that I may speak boldly, as I ought to.
    ___ Acts 4:13   c. We have boldness and confidence through faith.
    ___ Acts 4:29   d. The righteous are bold as a lion.
    ___ Ephesians 3:12   e. We are bold in God to speak the gospel of God.
    ___ Ephesians 6:19–20   f. You made me bold with strength in my soul.
    ___ Philippians 1:20   g. The disciples were bold; they had been with Jesus.
    ___ 1 Thessalonians 2:2 h. We shall not be ashamed, but have all boldness.

Failing the Test

The disciples weren't any different. Sure, they eventually became fearless witnesses, and ultimately all of them died for their faith or were persecuted, tortured, or exiled because of it. But they weren't always so bold. On the night of Jesus' betrayal—at the most important point in His life—every one of them fled for their lives, leaving Christ all alone (Mark 14:50).

He had been dropping hints all night. And it wasn't that the disciples were clueless. No, they'd seen how somber their teacher was. The Passover was a major fiesta time, and yet much of what He'd said to them that evening was A-list material for how to ruin a party. Imminent death. Broken bodies. Spilled blood. Deception. They weren't accustomed to seeing Him like this. Either Jesus was seriously depressed or something strange was going on. And it just got worse as the evening wore on. By the time the group reached the Garden, Jesus poured on the gloom and doom.

Although Christ had told them repeatedly that He would be betrayed and murdered, his words about someone within the group betraying Him were news to them. Surely not! They loved Him. They'd followed Him through thick and thin for more than three years now. So when He topped it off by saying that *every one of them* would falter in the face of opposition that very night, it was bordering on the sheer ridiculous. It seemed impossible.

Here's the truth: left to ourselves, apart from divine grace, we all lack the strength and fortitude to stand up for Christ in the face of hostility.

2. It had never occurred to the disciples that they would be put into a position to deny knowing their teacher and Lord.

   What had Jesus already cautioned them about in Matthew 10:33?

   _____

   _____

   _____

   According to 2 Timothy 2:12, what is our reward if we don't deny Jesus? What happens if we deny Him?

   _____

   _____

   _____

   We most often think of denying Jesus as a verbal act, but what does Titus 1:16 include as part of denying God?

   _____

   _____

   _____

It had never occurred to the disciples that they would be put into a position to deny knowing their teacher and Lord.

Since the disciples firmly believed Jesus was the Son of God, you'd think they might have received His words as a gentle warning. In an ideal world, their response would've been to fall on their faces and plead with God for grace and strength to endure the trial. Instead, the disciples seemed to respond by trying to fortify their own self-confidence by arrogantly declaring their loyalty to Jesus. "Not me, Lord. I'd never desert you!"

If they were on *Jeopardy*, they would've gotten the buzzer. Wrong answer. Sorry, no parting gifts. The disciples immediately relied upon their own strength. They swore to their own loyalty, bolstering their belief in themselves through empty promises and tooting their own horns about how they were prepared to suffer for Christ's sake.

They were about to be proven mistaken. Dead wrong. And for the rest of their lives, they'd never forget the decision they made to run from Jesus. It would be the most shameful moment of their lives, forever etched in their memories.

"Before the rooster crows, you will deny Me three times."

—Luke 22:61 NKJV

3. The disciples' arrogance was soon to be brought down to shame. "The lofty looks of man shall be humbled. The haughtiness of men shall be bowed down" (Isa. 2:11 NKJV). Jesus had prayed "that your faith should not fail; and when you have returned to Me, strengthen your brethren" (Luke 22:32 NKJV). These New Testament Scriptures do just that. Take a look at these verses, which encourage believers not to be ashamed of their Lord.

   Romans 1:16 — "I am not _____ of the _____ of _____, for it is the _____ of God to _____ for _____ who _____" (NKJV).

2 Timothy 1:8 — "Do not be _____ of the _____ of our _____" (NKJV).

2 Timothy 2:15 — "Be _____ to present yourself _____ to God, a _____ who does not need to be _____" (NKJV).

1 Peter 4:16 — "If anyone _____ as a _____, let him not be _____, but let him _____ God in this matter" (NKJV).

Pride Goes Before the Fall

Jesus had warned them of their cowardice earlier in the evening. Now as they reached the Garden, He cautioned them in more explicit terms. Once again He told Peter, "Assuredly, I say to you that this night, before the rooster crows, you will deny Me three times" (Matt. 26:34 NKJV). But Peter and the disciples seemed to completely miss the seriousness of what was about to occur. Their egos were severely bruised by the suggestion that they would abandon Christ in the hour of trial. They were so busy protesting Jesus' lack of confidence in them that they weren't really listening to Him. And it caused them to miss the entire point.

Jesus wasn't pointing the finger and saying, "You wimps. You won't even be able to stand against the wind when it blows. Why have I bothered keeping you around anyway?" Instead, He warned them for their own sake. He hated to see them take such a crippling spiritual blow, knowing the moment would haunt them for life. And so He warned them . . . "Listen guys, you're about to encounter a faith-testing time. Hold fast, 'cause this could really rattle you."

Unfortunately, the disciples remained oblivious to Jesus' tender warnings. Their sinful pride and self-sufficiency kept them blind. But they were about to learn the dangers of pride the hard way.

4. Pride affects us all on an hourly basis. That's why King Solomon, the wisest man ever, had so much to say about it. Check out the following Proverbs, and match up these familiar verses with his words about this lethal sin.

   ___ Proverbs 8:13   a. Pride goes before destruction.
   ___ Proverbs 11:2   b. By pride comes nothing but strife.
   ___ Proverbs 13:10   c. The Lord hates pride and arrogance.
   ___ Proverbs 16:18   d. A man's pride will bring him low.
   ___ Proverbs 29:23   e. When pride comes, shame follows.

Jesus wasn't pointing the finger and saying, "You wimps. You won't even be able to stand against the wind when it blows. Why have I bothered keeping you around anyway?"

Peter said to Him, "Even if I have to die with You, I will not deny You!"

—Matthew 26:35 NKJV

5. The disciples were completely unprepared for the trial they would face that night. Scripture often speaks of our need to be prepared—of having a prepared heart.

What did the people prepare their hearts to do in 2 Chronicles 19:3?

_____

_____

What did Jotham prepare in 2 Chronicles 27:6?

_____

_____

In Ezra 7:10, what do we find the scribe preparing his heart to do?

_____

_____

_____

What did John the Baptist prepare, according to the last part of Luke 1:17?

_____

_____

_____

> "Assuredly, I say to you that this night, before the rooster crows, you will deny Me three times."
>
> —Matt. 26:34 NKJV

Everybody Needs a Little Reassurance

What kind of leader are you when all your followers end up deserting you? That's the argument some people make in "proving" that Jesus was a lousy teacher (as if that would somehow vilify His being the Son of God . . . but that's another thing). Yet every one of the Gospel writers included Jesus' prediction of the disciples's denial—maybe to automatically refute that lame argument. Jesus had warned His followers; it was inexcusable that they were caught off-guard. And yet He knew perfectly well what was about to happen. In fact, His sovereignty is shown even more by His disciples's stubbornness. His faithfulness is shown in stark contrast to their unfaithfulness. God didn't include this in the Bible as a big, fat "Ha! I told you so!" The Scripture writers were merely showing *yet another* detail of this incredible night that pointed to the majesty of Jesus, further proving that this wasn't a man-made event. This was God allowing His Son to die.

Within a short time, everything Jesus had predicted would come to pass. And though the disciples would feel as if their entire universe was suddenly spinning out of control, Jesus kept reminding them that everything was proceeding according to God's plan.

> Within a short time, everything Jesus had predicted would come to pass.

"'I will strike the Shepherd, and the sheep of the flock will be scattered'" (Matt. 26:31 NKJV). It was a prophecy from Zechariah 13:7, spoken more than five hundred years before Christ. But notice Jesus' words to the disciples. Immediately after citing the prophecy about scattering the sheep, He adds a touch of encouragement: "But after I have been raised, I will go before you to Galilee" (verse 32).

What a crazy time to say this! The disciples were still reeling from the last prediction about their running at the drop of a hat. But again these words reflect the comforting heart of Jesus, even to those who in a few moments would deny Him. He wanted to reassure them that, yes, they would flee Him . . . but He was still in control.

6. Jesus provided reassurance to His followers, though His words didn't sink in until later. In the same way, He provides reassurance to us. What do each of these verses tell us about a Christian's assurance?

Colossians 2:2 —

_____

_____

_____

1 Thessalonians 1:5 —

_____

_____

_____

Hebrews 6:11 —

_____

_____

_____

Hebrews 10:22 —

_____

_____

_____

As everything else Christ said that night, the words of encouragement were lost on the disciples at that moment. Later they would remember what He had said and their faith would be strengthened. They had seen Him raise the dead on several occasions before this. They were present when He raised Lazarus and told Martha, "I am the resurrection and the life" (John 11:25 NKJV). Eventually, this would all click in their heads. But for now they were too wigged out to make sense of what He meant. The weird vibes from Jesus all night. The macabre words about dying. The stinging words accusing them of running away. It was too much.

DOWN IN THE DUMPS

You can't blame the disciples for being discouraged. Obviously, this night was turning into a nightmare. But nothing else with Jesus had gone the way they'd hoped either. Jesus had always talked about God's Kingdom. And so they expected a massive overthrow, with Jesus on an earthly throne, His dominion centered in Israel, and His Kingdom sweeping across the globe. Instead, they remained a little band of nobodies, ill-equipped, rejected, and seemingly going nowhere. Now with their head honcho being arrested in the middle of the night, things didn't seem too hopeful. Whatever Jesus had planned for building His Kingdom, surely it didn't include this night. —*Ashamed of the Gospel*

I Don't Know Him

Fast-forward a few hours. Jesus is inside the high priest's house on trial for His life. Peter is desperate to see what's going on inside but restricted to loitering outside in the courtyard. He, too, is facing the trial of his life, but in a different sense. On this infamous final night of Jesus' earthly ministry, Peter will experience utter failure.

During that dark night of Peter's trial, although his courage and devotion failed when put to the test, his faith in Christ did not. And that's what distinguishes Peter's temporary defection (and that of the other disciples) from Judas' treachery. Judas deliberately rejected Christ. His actions were premeditated and full of disbelief and hatred. He was through with this "Son of God" talk and wanted to put Christ in His place.

Peter's denial, on the other hand, was a spur-of-the-moment act of weak-hearted cowardice. Despite denying Jesus publicly, he still had faith in Him. And that's what broke Peter's heart—that he could say one thing and believe another.

7. We don't always do as we should. Despite our best intentions, we end up falling on our faces when it comes to emulating Christ's life. Paul understood this dilemma all too well. What did he say in Romans 7:15?

_____

_____

_____

During that dark night of Peter's trial, although his courage and devotion failed when put to the test, his faith in Christ did not.

Peter was admitted to the courtyard during the initial phase of the trial—while Jesus was still in Annas's house. It was almost immediately after his admission to the courtyard that he denied Christ for the first time. Apparently the young girl who served as the high priest's doorkeeper had her eye on Peter when he entered the courtyard and was suspicious or curious about him, so she went over by the fire for a closer look. She studied his face until she was confident of who Peter was.

"When he had gone out to the gateway, another girl saw him and said to those who were there, 'This fellow also was with Jesus of Nazareth.' But again he denied with an oath, 'I do not know the Man!'" (Matt. 26:71–72 NKJV). To the whole group who pressed Peter to admit that he was one of the Twelve, "He denied it and said, 'I am not!'" (John 18:25 NKJV). And so for the second time since entering the courtyard, Peter denied even knowing Jesus.

It's ironic that a couple of servant girls and a small group of household servants could elicit such an emphatic denial from Peter. Remember that only hours before this, he had insisted that he would *never* deny Christ, even if it cost him his life. In the Garden, he'd had the guts to draw his sword against a large group of armed men. But now he was cowering and fearful because a couple of young girls identified him as a follower of Jesus.

DID YA KNOW?

The cursing and swearing aren't what you're thinking (don't go down that road). This means something different today than it did back in Jesus' day. In this case, Peter pronounced a curse on himself, expressing a hope that he would die violently at God's own hand if his words were untrue. And then he swore yet another oath—calling again on God to be his witness—that he didn't know Jesus. It was the strongest sort of oath you could take. When a person took such an oath and then used it to cover a lie, it amounted to the absolute worst kind of lie. It compounded the original lie with an overt blasphemy, suggesting God would be witness to a lie—and calling the judgment of God down on one's own head in the process.

Sometime during that hour, Caiaphas succeeded in eliciting the testimony from Jesus that the Sanhedrin deemed blasphemous. Mark places the beating, blindfolding, and spitting on Jesus prior to Peter's denial (Mark 14:64–66), so Peter probably witnessed the abuse Jesus suffered. Can you imagine what he must've been thinking? Meanwhile, the group in the courtyard may have been talking among themselves about Peter and his relationship to Jesus. They finally decided to confront him with evidence of why they were certain he was one of Jesus' disciples: "And a little later those who stood by came up and said to Peter, 'Surely you also are one of them, for your speech betrays you'" (Matt. 26:73 NKJV). Luke says the accuser on this

> "When he had gone out to the gateway, another girl saw him and said to those who were there, 'This fellow also was with Jesus of Nazareth.' But again he denied with an oath, 'I do not know the Man!'"
>
> —Matt. 26:71–72 NKJV

occasion "*confidently* affirmed, saying, 'Surely this fellow also was with Him, for he is a Galilean'" (Luke 22:59 NKJV, *emphasis added*).

Their accusation seems to have rattled Peter severely. This time "he began to curse and swear, saying, 'I do not know the Man!'" (Matt. 26:74 NKJV). By this time, Peter seems to have thrown out virtually everything Jesus had taught him the past few years. He was now so desperate to confirm his own lie that he abandoned all restraint. "Immediately, while he was still speaking, the rooster crowed" (Luke 22:60 NKJV).

DID YA KNOW?

Mark no doubt learned of the incident from Peter himself. (Mark's Gospel was even referred to in the early church as "the memoirs of Peter" because Peter was obviously the primary human source of the unique details Mark recorded.) Peter himself might have wished to emphasize that the rooster crowed twice because it showed how patient the Lord had been with him, giving him so many warning signals and tokens of His grace—even while Peter persisted to deny Jesus and basically spit in His face.

Jesus must've been positioned precisely where He could turn and look out an open window and into Peter's eyes.

It was precisely at the moment of the second rooster-crowing that (according to Luke) "The Lord turned and looked at Peter. Then Peter remembered the word of the Lord, how He had said to him, 'Before the rooster crows, you will deny Me three times'" (Luke 22:61 NKJV). Jesus must've been positioned precisely where He could turn and look out an open window and into Peter's eyes. His already battered face, so recently beaten and spat upon by his accusers, turned in that instant toward Peter, and His loving but all-knowing eyes met Peter's eyes and stared into his very soul. It wasn't an accusing glare, but a tender, piercing look that broke Peter's heart.

Jesus understood Peter's dilemma. He knew his denial wasn't a hard-hearted rejection of Him as Judas's betrayal had been! For this reason, after Jesus' resurrection, He specifically sought out Peter and forgave him in the presence of the other disciples. He then commissioned him anew for service (John 21:15–17).

It's an incredible portrait of Jesus' overwhelming love. At the moment when He was being unjustly spat upon and mocked by his enemies, when He needed just a sign—even a word—of encouragement, His closest friends deserted Him. Even more, Peter flat-out denied that he ever knew Jesus. Yet the Lord saw, had compassion, forgave—and fully restored His beloved friend.

The final chapter of Peter's story is a great triumph, not a defeat. He ends up becoming a fearless preacher, a powerful church leader, and an unforgotten martyr for Christ. But let's go back to that fateful night for Peter—a chapter of stunning defeat—not to drive a stake in his heart, but because his decisions can teach us all vital lessons in our faith.

How did Peter fall? How could he go from Jesus' most outspoken follower to His most outspoken stranger—in just a few hours' time? It's important to see that Peter's failure didn't just occur spontaneously. He repeatedly took the wrong steps that put him on the pathway to failure. To shed light on those specific mishaps, let's take a deeper look at Peter's personality.

He Talked Too Much

Peter often acted as spokesperson for the whole group. He was a type-A personality who was naturally loud, opinionated, and outspoken—great characteristics for a group leader. But these traits also made him prone to reckless impulsiveness. He frequently spoke before he thought. On a few occasions, he was even so brash as to contradict Jesus (Mark 8:32). And he wasn't the greatest listener. He was often oblivious as to when he should be listening rather than sounding off. To make matters worse, Peter sometimes neglected to learn from his own mistakes. Even after Jesus corrected him, he remained slow to hear and quick to speak. You'd think with all his bitter experience, he would know by then not to argue with Christ. After all, Jesus had never been wrong about anything.

But right up to the night of Jesus' betrayal, when Jesus tried to forewarn Peter and the disciples that they were about to stumble, Peter not only argued with Jesus, but he kept pressing the point even after Jesus corrected him. "Jesus said to him, 'Assuredly, I say to you that this night, before the rooster crows, you will deny Me three times.' Peter said to Him, 'Even if I have to die with You, I will not deny You!'" (Matt. 26:34–35 NKJV).

There was simply no talking to Peter about it. He brashly assumed he knew his own heart even better than Jesus did. He kept right on insisting that he would never fall away, even if he were the last person in the world left standing for Christ. But all the good intentions in the world do not equal real virtue. Boasting is no true measure of boldness. In fact, Peter's braggadocio proved only his folly, not his faithfulness.

> Peter often let his mouth lead the way, which sometimes got him in trouble.

8. Peter often let his mouth lead the way, which sometimes got him in trouble. The Book of James specifically mentions the dangers of the tongue and its disruptiveness.

   According to James 3:6, what is the tongue like?

   _____

   _____

   _____

   As Christians, what does James 1:26 warn us about?

   _____

   _____

   _____

Why do you think the Bible is so harsh on what comes out of our mouths?

_____

_____

_____

He Prayed Too Little

Peter also botched it because he neglected prayer. Prayer was the one thing that could've strengthened Peter to face the temptation the Lord had forewarned him about. But having already scorned Jesus' warning about his imminent failure, Peter had no sense of his desperate need to pray for God to strengthen him.

9. How would you characterize your own commitment to prayer? Check any and all of the boxes that apply.

❑ I pray constantly. Prayer is as necessary to my day as the very air I breathe.

❑ I pray regularly. I have a daily prayer time when I meet with God.

❑ I pray intermittently. Here a little, there a little. I pray when I think of it.

❑ I pray routinely. Wouldn't start a meal without it.

❑ I pray occasionally. I don't say "no" when I'm called upon to lead in prayer.

❑ I pray systematically. I have a list, and I keep a record of answered prayers.

❑ I pray sporadically. I send up quick, desperate prayers when I am in need.

❑ I pray when absolutely necessary. When there's nothing else I can do, I turn to God in prayer.

Ninety-nine point nine percent of the problems and failures Christians face are directly related to prayerlessness. "You do not have because you do not ask" (James 4:2 NKJV). Perhaps Peter's failure could've been avoided if he had spent that time in the Garden praying for the grace to endure. But Peter and the other disciples were so physically exhausted after a long and difficult day that it's possible they didn't even realize how much their spiritual strength was depleted.

He Slept Too Much

Peter's not the only one guilty of this charge. The entire group was exhausted, including Jesus. But rather than follow Christ's request to keep watch and pray, Peter and the gang succumbed to the land of snooze. Unfortunately, this was yet another factor in Peter's downfall. He was sound asleep when the soldiers first arrived to take Jesus. Peter was probably still shaking off the cobwebs when he impulsively drew his

> "You do not have because you do not ask."
>
> —James 4:2 NKJV

> Prayer was the one thing that could've strengthened Peter to face the temptation the Lord had forewarned him about.

sword and struck Malchus, the high priest's servant. It wasn't the action of someone who was wide awake and at the peak of his sensibilities—definitely not someone who'd been with Jesus, the ultimate peacemaker, for three-plus years.

10. The disciples should've been on their guard since Jesus had warned them more than once that night. Their neglect left them vulnerable to attack.

How is God described in Isaiah 52:12?

_____

_____

_____

What guards our hearts, according to Philippians 4:7?

_____

_____

_____

Who guards us, according to 2 Thessalonians 3:3?

_____

_____

_____

> Believers are reminded again and again throughout the New Testament to watch and pray.

There's nothing inherently wrong with sleep. It's a necessary, God-ordained function that our bodies require. But Christ often spoke about the importance of feeding our spirits more than our bodies. We are spiritual beings contained in fleshly bodies, living in a spiritual world. Everything of this culture says otherwise. It tells us to feed our desires, whatever form they may be. It preaches the message of instant gratification. If it "feels good," then just do it.

The gospel of Christ stands in stark contrast to the world's message. (Gee, what's new?) And the disciples heard this message firsthand, yet still fell to the call of the flesh. Despite seeing Jesus sweating blood and agonizing in prayer, they decided to sleep. Despite His repeatedly waking them and asking them to pray for Him, they chose to doze.

The result? They were unprepared for the night's events. Physically, they were groggy. But more important, they were spiritually disoriented and unfit to face the heavenly battle that had already begun in the Garden. Ultimately, Peter's spiritual dullness led to his rash decisions that he would regret for the rest of his life.

11. Believers are reminded again and again throughout the New Testament to watch and pray.

Matthew 24:42 — "_____ therefore, for you do not know _____ _____ your _____ is _____" (NKJV).

Mark 13:33 — "Take heed, _____ and _____; for you do not know when the time is" (NKJV).

Luke 21:36 — "_____ therefore, and _____ _____ that you may be counted _____ . . . " (NKJV)

1 Thessalonians 5:6 — "Therefore let us not _____, as others do, but let us _____ and be _____" (NKJV).

He Acted Too Fast

Peter believed in himself. He had a self-confidence matched only by his outspokenness. It's likely that his boasting that night (when Christ suggested that he would deny Him) had him riled up. He was determined to prove his faithfulness. So it's no wonder that when finally put to the test, he tried to take matters into his own hands and rely on carnal force. When the temple officers tried to apprehend Jesus, Peter "stretched out his hand and drew his sword, struck the servant of the high priest, and cut off his ear" (Matt. 26:51 NKJV).

It was an impulsive and reckless thing to do. Obviously, if Jesus wanted to resist or avoid arrest, He certainly had the ability to do so. But Peter always seemed to think he knew better, even though doing things his own way never got him anywhere but deeper into trouble.

Christ had repeatedly foretold His own arrest and death. In fact, one time, when Peter told Jesus His words about dying were crazy talk, Peter got an earful—his Master called him "Satan" (Matt. 16:23 NKJV). Ouch. You'd think Peter might've taken note of that one. Instead, he was the first to draw swords that night in the Garden.

Peter's actions were rash. And the Lord let him know it. His rebuke as He healed Malchus's ear no doubt wounded Peter's pride even more painfully than his own sword had wounded Malchus. And since Peter's courage and self-confidence were completely rooted in carnal pride, once his pride was deflated, he had no reserves from which he could draw strength. He might as well split with the other disciples.

12. The Bible warns us against setting our hearts on earthly things.

   What effect do earthly things have on the establishing of God's Word in our hearts, according to Mark 4:19?

   _____

   _____

   _____

In Philippians 3:19, how does Paul describe people who have their minds set on earthly things?

_____

_____

_____

What is the message of Colossians 3:2?

_____

_____

_____

In 1 John 2:15, what does the Beloved Disciple warn against?

_____

_____

_____

We can't teeter on the line between living as Christians and blending in with everyone else. Following Jesus is an all-or-nothing deal.

He Followed Too Far

Peter's final step toward failure was the decision to follow Christ from a distance after abandoning Him. He tried to stay far enough away so that no one would suspect he was a disciple of Jesus, yet close enough to be able to see what was happening. The strategy led Peter right into the place where he would be tempted the most—the courtyard of the high priest—and at just the time when he was least prepared to handle such a temptation.

His method is still used today by those afraid of confessing their Christian faith. They try to blend in as much as possible with the world so no one will point them out. They hang out with non-Christians not because they have lofty aspirations to evangelize or befriend others in the name of Christ, but simply because they don't want to be seen. The reality is, however, that those people are in far more spiritual danger because they're trying to conceal their relationship with Jesus. Big mistake, as Peter found out the hard way.

13. We can't teeter on the line between living as Christians and blending in with everyone else. Following Jesus is an all-or-nothing deal. We must choose one or the other—darkness or light.

What does Jesus say about those who follow Him in John 8:12?

_____

_____

_____

In Ephesians 5:8, how does Paul describe our lives before we met Jesus compared to after we came to know the Lord?

_____

_____

_____

Where should we walk as we follow after Jesus, according to 1 John 1:7?

_____

_____

_____

Not So Different

It's easy to read about Peter's mistake and point the finger. After all, it was his choice to cut off a servant's ear in rage. It was his choice to flee Jesus. And it was his choice to lie about knowing Christ.

But the lesson goes deeper than learning how to not repeat Peter's blunders. It's a humbling truth, one that cuts to the core of all of us. You ready for it? Here goes:

You're just like Peter. Me too. We all are, to various degrees.

Even if you're not the loud-mouth Peter was, haven't you ever stuck your foot in your mouth out of self-confidence? Maybe you're known as being level-headed, but undoubtedly at one point your rash actions have caused nothing but headaches. And did you know that every time we fail to defend the name of Christ—and all that He is—in the face of a God-hating world, we're playing the role of Peter? We've all denied Jesus more than we'll ever know. So for all Peter's faults, we are never in the place to judge him, lest we be judged ourselves (turn to any page in the New Testament and you'll find that point).

But there's good news. Just as Peter found redemption from Christ, so do we. Upon Jesus' return to the disciples (after being resurrected), He made a point to restore Peter's faith. He acknowledged his failure, but He also moved on, encouraging Peter to greater things. And great things he certainly did as the "rock" on which Jesus founded His church (Matt. 16:18 NKJV).

Likewise, Jesus is well aware of the times we've failed Him. And no matter how severe we think our mistake or how convinced we are that God could never forgive us, Jesus comes to do exactly that. He's ready to move on, ready to forgive us and restore us. But part of that restoration means learning from our mistakes. Peter learned his lesson, and he grew into a fearless witness for the life and testimony of Christ. He wasn't ashamed and didn't hold back in front of anyone. In fact, later Peter would face the exact same crowd that plotted Jesus' death—Annas, Caiaphas, the whole Sanhedrin crew. This time, he didn't waver. When told to shut up, he gave the classic response: "We cannot but speak the things which we have seen and heard" (Acts 4:20 NKJV). In other words, Peter didn't care what anyone thought; this time he was going to respond right.

Just as Peter found redemption from Christ, so do we.

14. So . . . what's your response?

_____

_____

_____

Wrapping It Up

Hours before Peter's denial, Christ had prayed, "Those whom You gave Me I have kept; and none of them is lost except the son of perdition [Judas], that the Scripture might be fulfilled" (John 17:12 NKJV). Jesus knew Peter would stumble, but He also knew that Peter would repent and be restored after his failure—just as He knew Judas's treachery grew out of a final, irremediable rejection of the truth. Both Peter's repentance and Judas's apostasy were in perfect accord with the plan and purposes of God. Peter truly belonged to Christ, and therefore Christ Himself kept Peter from stumbling so badly that he would be destroyed.

Things to Remember

- Left to ourselves, apart from divine grace, we all lack the strength and fortitude to stand up for Christ in the face of hostility.
- Rather than trying to motivate the disciples to summon courage and self-confidence, Jesus was reminding them of their weakness and urging them to seek His strength.
- The disciples' egos were severely wounded by the suggestion that they would abandon Christ in the hour of trial.
- Although Peter's courage and devotion failed when put to the test, his faith in Christ did not fail.
- Unfortunately, Peter didn't always know when to listen and when to be quiet.
- All the good intentions in the world do not equal real virtue.
- Peter's courage and self-confidence were completely rooted in carnal pride, so once his pride was deflated, he had no reserves from which he could draw strength.
- It's easy to read about Peter's mistake and point the finger. But the humbling truth is that we're all like Peter, to various degrees. We've all denied Jesus more than we'll ever know.
- Just as Peter found redemption from Christ, so do we.

Memorize This!

*Be diligent to present yourself approved to God,
a worker who does not need to be ashamed.*
—2 Timothy 2:15 NKJV

Check This Out

If you want to find out more about the following related topics, check out John MacArthur's extensive resources in the *MacArthur LifeWorks Library CD-ROM*, or visit www.gty.org.

✠ Denying Christ
✠ Enduring persecution
✠ Peer pressure
✠ Hiding your faith
✠ Failure
✠ Lack of prayer
✠ Fence-sitting faith
✠ Impulsiveness
✠ Boasting
✠ Pride

Notes

Lesson 6
A Mock Trial

All day they twist my words; all their thoughts are against me for evil.
—Psalm 56:5 NKJV

The Word to the Wise

Before starting this lesson, read Matthew 26:57–68.

For Starters

Jesus was exhausted, for sure. It was long past midnight, yet there would be no rest for Him this night. The mob hustled Him straight to the high priest's house—bound, beaten, and brought before men who were ready to pounce on Him. It was a complete scam. The charges were trumped up. The witnesses were paid to lie. Everyone there hated Him. And throughout this mockery of justice, Christ remained alone. No one aided Him. No one defended Him. He wouldn't even defend Himself, though He had every right to prove them all liars. In the face of their illegal maneuverings and murderous intentions, Jesus stood silent and trusted in His Father's sovereign plan.

"You shall appoint judges . . . and they shall judge the people with just judgment."

—Deuteronomy 16:18 NKJV

Hand-Delivered by God

What do you think of when you hear the word *justice*? A courtroom? A judge? Martin Luther King Jr.? For everyone in the United States, justice is a premise of life, whether we realize it or not. It allows us to walk down the street with confidence, knowing that if we're attacked, our attacker will pay the price when caught. Justice upholds the law. It's a system by which fairness and rightness reign.

For hundreds of years, the Israelites lived under a system of justice given straight from God. Talk about the ultimate judge! God established laws for His chosen people and He gave them to Moses. Israel's justice system ensured maximum fairness and encouraged mercy. In fact, it was far superior to any known on earth. It upheld fairness stronger than any of the Canaanite standards and was more advanced and more equitable than the Egyptian system of governing. In fact, most of our modern system of justice has been derived from the same Law handed to Moses—almost thirty-five hundred years ago!

What do you think of when you hear the word justice?

1. What was the secret to Israel's system? Check out the principles God established in Deuteronomy 16:18–20.

_____

_____

_____

> "You shall not pervert justice; you shall not show partiality, nor take a bribe, for a bribe blinds the eyes of the wise and twists the words of the righteous."
>
> —Deuteronomy 16:19 NKJV

"You shall appoint _____ and _____ in all your gates, which the LORD your God gives you, according to your tribes, and they shall _____ the people with _____ _____. You shall not _____ justice; you shall not show _____, nor take a _____, for a _____ _____ the eyes of the wise and _____ the _____ of the righteous. You shall follow what is _____ _____, that you may live and inherit the land which the LORD your God is giving you." (NKJV)

2. God is just, and He called upon His people to act justly. Match up these verses on justice.

___ Deuteronomy 32:4   a. God loves righteousness and justice.
___ Job 34:4   b. A disreputable witness scorns justice.
___ Psalm 33:5   c. Seek justice.
___ Psalm 106:3   d. All God's ways are just. He is without injustice.
___ Psalm 111:7   e. Blessed are those who keep justice.
___ Proverbs 19:28   f. Do justly, love mercy, walk humbly.
___ Proverbs 21:3   g. The works of God's hands are verity and just.
___ Isaiah 1:17   h. Let us choose justice for ourselves.
___ Micah 6:8   i. Doing justice is more acceptable than sacrifice.

DID YA KNOW?

The Great Sanhedrin was patterned after the council of elders Moses convened in Numbers 11:16: "The LORD said to Moses: 'Gather to Me seventy men of the elders of Israel, whom you know to be the elders of the people and officers over them; bring them to the tabernacle of meeting, that they may stand there with you'"(NKJV). Those seventy men, plus Moses, formed a council of seventy-one elders whose job it was to govern the Israelites in the wilderness.

> "You shall follow what is altogether just."
>
> —Deuteronomy 16:20 NKJV

The Sanhedrin

Sometime between the Old and New Testaments, the Great Sanhedrin was established in Jerusalem as the highest court in Israel. By Jesus' time, the Sanhedrin had become a joke. It was completely corrupt with men who governed with their own political agendas. You could buy your way into the council with political favors or even money. Once in, members jostled for position by forming cliques. Those who didn't play the game were left out.

Because Rome ruled Israel at that time, its government ultimately controlled the high priesthood. Things became so bad that both the high priest and the ruling priests of the temple (known as Sadducees) openly denied the supernatural elements of the Old Testament in order to gain favor with local Roman leaders. The Sanhedrin frequently made decisions that were politically motivated. In fact, the plan to do away with Christ wasn't just because they hated His teachings; they were also scared of His increasing influence among the Jewish population.

3. The Sanhedrin was often motivated by political ambition, greed, and selfishness in its decisions. Instead of ruling justly, these men let partiality dictate their decisions.

   How does this stand in opposition to God's character?

   _____

   _____

   _____

   Why do you think God allowed this?

   _____

   _____

   _____

Strict Guidelines for Justice

Despite the corruption within the Sanhedrin, the justice system was still governed by rules of evidence and principles of impartiality that had been established under Moses. Two credible witnesses were still required to establish guilt. The accused were supposed to be entitled to a public trial. People placed on trial were entitled to a defense, including the right to call witnesses and present evidence.

4. As a way to stop anyone from bringing false testimony against an accused person, Moses' Law had strict procedures and harsh consequences. According to Deuteronomy 19:16–19, what was the punishment for those who lied on the "witness stand"?

_____

_____

_____

There were additional rules the Jewish leaders followed—specific rules that assured a fair case for anyone accused of a crime. A full day of fasting had to be observed by the council between the passing of a sentence and the execution of the criminal. After the obligatory day of fasting, council members were polled again to see if they had changed their opinions. Guilty verdicts could be overturned, but a not-guilty verdict couldn't be taken back. In other words, an accused person was given the benefit of the doubt—and then some.

Fasting wasn't the only way the Sanhedrin ensured fairness in capital cases:

- The council could only try cases where an outside party had brought the charges. If charges had been brought against the accused by council members, the entire council was disqualified from trying the case.

- Testimony of all witnesses had to be precise as to the date, time, and location of the event being considered.

- Women, children, slaves, and the mentally incompetent weren't allowed to testify. (Remember, this was a different culture and time.)

- Anyone of questionable character wasn't allowed to stand as a witness. (Can you imagine if this were practiced today?)

- The accused was to be presumed innocent until an official guilty verdict was reached.

- Criminal trials couldn't be held at night. If a trial was already underway when nighttime fell, court was to be recessed until the following day.

> "The LORD your God is God of gods and Lord of lords, the great God, mighty and awesome, who shows no partiality nor takes a bribe."
>
> —Deuteronomy 10:17 NKJV

Fairness Forgotten?

Now think about Jesus' "trial" before the Sanhedrin. *Every one* of these elements and procedures wasn't just overlooked, it was completely thrown out the window! His trial was unjust and illegal by virtually every principle of jurisprudence known at the time. Anyone with half a brain could've walked into the room and called a mistrial. And yet that night, Caiaphas and the Sanhedrin turned their own council into a kangaroo court with the predetermined purpose of killing Jesus. Justice received a royal kick in the face.

The Jewish leaders had a plan. Jesus was taken to the former high priest Annas's house so he could listen to Jesus' side of the story. The Sanhedrin expected Jesus to give an account of His teaching, and then Annas (who, remember, was also Caiaphas's father-in-law) would decide what kind of charge to file. He had several options at his disposal. He could charge Jesus with blasphemy, a crime punishable by death under Jewish law. Since Jesus had said many things in His public ministry that the Jewish leaders deemed blasphemous, that seemed the most likely charge.

5. What claim had Jesus made in John 5:18 that caused an uproar among the religious leaders?

_____

_____

_____

Here was the problem: the Romans had to authorize and carry out any execution. So it was rare for them to approve the death penalty for blasphemy (which wasn't as big of a deal to them as it was to the Jews). Because of that, Annas tried to find a way to charge Jesus with sedition or insurrection. John records that Annas "asked Jesus about His disciples and His doctrine" (John 18:19 NKJV). In effect, Jesus was being brought before a court to answer charges, even though He hadn't even been charged with a specific offense. This was completely out of order and contrary to every standard of fair jurisprudence. On top of that, Annas was trying to get Jesus to incriminate Himself—something also contrary to the principles of justice that were supposed to govern the Sanhedrin.

For there is no partiality with God.

—Romans 2:11 NKJV

A Circus Court

Jesus, of course, was above this charade. Exasperated and still unable to find anything he could charge Jesus with, Annas finally had Him bound and sent Him to Caiaphas's house, where members of the Sanhedrin were already assembled for the trial. Most likely, the council was embarrassed when Jesus entered this second house with still no charges against Him. But it didn't stop them. They already had false witnesses who were prepared to testify against Jesus.

Yet another rule in the justice system prohibited the council from soliciting anyone's testimony. They were supposed to be acting as impartial judges, not prosecuting attorneys. By openly asking for damaging testimony against Jesus, they forfeited any perception of impartiality. But they were desperate. They were determined to press the issue against Jesus until they found even a single believable complaint against Him—even if it meant destroying their credibility that night.

6. The Sanhedrin had set up an entire scam to convict Jesus. Read Matthew 26:59–60 and Mark 14:56. What ended up happening?

_____

_____

_____

Get this: the Jewish leaders couldn't even find liars who were clever enough to fabricate a tale that agreed with the lies of others! They were making complete idiots of themselves. Can you imagine how red-faced these leaders were?

Finally, two false (and probably paid) witnesses came forward with the words the leaders wanted to hear. "We heard Him say, 'I will destroy this temple made with hands, and within three days I will build another made without hands'" (Mark 14:58 NKJV). The details of their separate stories still didn't quite jibe—but there were enough similarities in what they said to serve Caiaphas's purposes. Their testimonies could be twisted to suggest that Jesus was advocating the total overthrow of the Jewish religion (by replacing the current temple with another). And with that, the Sanhedrin could charge Him with high blasphemy for claiming that He could rebuild the temple by miraculous means ("without hands"—Mark 14:58 NKJV).

So You Think You're God, Huh?

Obviously, since the two witnesses' stories were incongruent, their testimony should've been automatically disallowed and the case against Jesus dismissed. But the Sanhedrin wasn't about to give up. They had already secretly determined to eliminate the threat they imagined Jesus posed to their power, and to do that, they needed credible evidence against Him. Now they seemed to have it—or at least these witnesses' testimony could be spun into something remotely resembling evidence that Jesus was guilty of blasphemy. And so "the high priest arose and said to Him, 'Do You answer nothing? What is it these men testify against You?'" (Matt. 26:62 NKJV).

7. Like many instances throughout Jesus' path to crucifixion, this moment had been prophesied hundreds of years before. How does Isaiah characterize Christ as He stands before His accusers in Isaiah 53:7?

_____

_____

_____

> The Jews sought all the more to kill Him, because He not only broke the Sabbath, but also said that God was His Father, making Himself equal with God.
>
> —John 5:18 NKJV

> "We heard Him say, 'I will destroy this temple made with hands, and within three days I will build another made without hands.'"
>
> —Mark 14:58 NKJV

Jesus responded with complete silence. Not a single word. Can't you picture Him looking directly into Caiaphas's eyes with such a quiet confidence? As the blameless Son of God, He had no obligation to testify against Himself. And just as He had done previously with Annas, He made that point with Caiaphas in a dramatic way—by simply declining to testify against Himself.

His silence was infuriating to the council. Surely He had *something* to say! The more He kept quiet, the angrier they got. Finally in frustration, Caiaphas yelled at Jesus: "I put You under oath by the living God: Tell us if You are the Christ, the Son of God!" (Matt. 26:63 NKJV). Obviously Caiaphas was familiar with Jesus' claims. He knew that Jesus had publicly "said that God was His Father, making Himself equal with God" (John 5:18 NKJV).

8. Blasphemy is one of two things: profaning God in word or deed, or actually claiming to be God.

Who did Jesus claim to be in John 4:25–26?

_____

_____

_____

Who did Jesus say He was in John 9:35–37?

_____

_____

_____

Such claims would have been considered blasphemy by the Sanhedrin. What was the punishment for a blasphemer, according to Leviticus 24:16?

_____

_____

_____

For many bore false witness against Him, but their testimonies did not agree.

—Mark 14:56 NKJV

But accusing Jesus of blasphemy was one thing; proving it was another. Caiaphas still needed credible testimony to prove that Jesus had ever said He was the Son of God. All he had were a few rumors and the flawed testimony of two witnesses. Caiaphas needed better evidence. And so he used a dirty trick. (Gee, what a surprise!) He placed Jesus under oath using God's name and demanded that He tell them whether or not He was Christ.

Jesus gave him precisely what he hoped for. He replied, "It is as you said. Nevertheless, I say to you, hereafter you will see the Son of Man sitting at the right hand of the Power, and coming on the clouds of heaven" (Matt. 26:64 NKJV). Mark records that Jesus furthermore used the name "I AM," which was the proper name by which God revealed Himself to Moses (Ex. 3:13–14), and a holy word the Jews were commanded never to say. It was a double-whammy for Jesus. And it was all Caiaphas needed to hear.

THAT'S NOT FAIR!

Jesus was executed as a criminal on a cross. The problem was, He hadn't committed a single crime—no stealing, no murder . . . nothing! He'd never even had an evil thought or spoken an evil word. Jesus' execution was the most unjust act ever perpetrated on a human being. Yet it shows us that even when a person is walking completely in God's will, he may still experience unjust suffering. Like Jesus, you may be misunderstood, misrepresented, hated, or even persecuted. But Jesus set the standard. And as a believer, you can follow His example of allowing God—and God alone—to defend you. —*Truth for Today*

He was oppressed and He was afflicted, yet He opened not His mouth.

—Isaiah 53:7 NKJV

A Predetermined Verdict

Matthew 26:65–66 says, "Then the high priest tore his clothes, saying, 'He has spoken blasphemy! What further need do we have of witnesses? Look, now you have heard His blasphemy! What do you think?'" (NKJV).

It's a disgusting scene. Here Caiaphas acts as if he were outraged over the gall of Jesus to utter God's holy name, much less equate Himself with God. But his melodrama is as artificial as a plastic doll. He wasn't upset that God's unspeakable name had been used; he was rejoicing inside that Jesus had finally said something he could use against Him. He now had the "evidence" he needed, and to his absolute delight there was no need for any more bumbling witnesses to ruin the scene with their conflicting stories. As far as he was concerned, Christ had blasphemed openly before the entire council. They all were witnesses against Him. His condemnation was now a done deal. The high priest immediately asked for a verdict from the council: "What do you think?"

They answered as if they were singing the chorus to their favorite song: "He is deserving of death" (Matt. 26:66 NKJV). And just like that, the council came up with a verdict: "They all condemned Him to be deserving of death" (Mark 14:64 NKJV). What a coincidence, huh? It was exactly the verdict they'd agreed upon *long before* they had ever heard His case.

"They all condemned Him to be deserving of death."

—Mark 14:64 NKJV

✠

DID YA KNOW?

The tearing of Caiaphas's clothes was supposed to signify his utter shock and outrage over an alleged act of open blasphemy. Tearing your clothes was an expression of extreme grief and shock from the most ancient biblical times (Gen. 37:34; Num. 14:6; 2 Sam. 1:11). However, the high priest was forbidden to tear his clothes (Lev. 21:10). So ironically, while Annas was theatrically faking a hissy-fit over Jesus' supposed act of blasphemy, he himself was actually committing a rather serious act of sacrilege, profaning the high priest's office in a way Scripture specifically forbids.

✠

The case was closed in their eyes. Jesus was guilty. They had the proof. Now the members of the Sanhedrin began to vent their hatred of Jesus openly. "They spat in His face and beat Him; and others struck Him with the palms of their hands, saying, 'Prophesy to us, Christ! Who is the one who struck You?'" (Matt. 26:67–68 NKJV). According to Luke, they blindfolded Him before striking Him and ordered Him to prophesy about who hit Him. Luke adds that there were "many other things they blasphemously spoke against Him" (Luke 22:65 NKJV). Ironically, blasphemy was the very crime they had accused Him of, but they themselves were the ones who were guilty of it. Here they were, mocking God to His face.

9. Can you imagine if you were in Jesus' shoes? Our first response would be to strike back or argue our case. This was the ultimate injustice. But Christ took every blow, every insult with an unfathomable quiet and majestic grace. How does 1 Peter 2:23 describe His behavior?

_____

_____

_____

> He was led as a lamb to the slaughter, and as a sheep before its shearers is silent, so He opened not His mouth.
>
> —Isaiah 53:7 NKJV

A Potential Snag

Despite their gloating over Jesus, the coast wasn't completely clear for the Sanhedrin. They needed a careful strategy in taking Jesus' case before the Roman officials. A few years prior to this, Rome had rescinded the Jewish leaders' right to carry out the death penalty on their own (John 18:31). All capital punishment now had to be approved and implemented by Roman authorities. If the Sanhedrin intended to ask Rome to execute the death penalty against Jesus, they'd have to present the case against Him in a compelling way. The decision was made immediately to take Jesus to Pontius

Pilate to get Roman permission to have Him put to death—preferably by Roman executioners. "They led Him away and delivered Him to Pontius Pilate the governor" (Matt. 27:2 NKJV).

DID YA KNOW?

The Sanhedrin constituted a religious court, not a civil one. Their jurisdiction covered matters directly pertaining to the Jewish religion. They had no authority to put anyone to death without prior Roman approval (John 18:31)—even in cases where Old Testament law prescribed death. That meant many Old Testament moral and religious standards couldn't be enforced with biblical penalties. The Romans rarely approved the death penalty in cases of adultery, homosexuality, blasphemy, false prophecy—or other moral or religious offenses.

> When He was reviled, [He] did not revile in return; when He suffered, He did not threaten, but committed Himself to Him who judges righteously.
>
> —1 Peter 2:23 NKJV

Trumped-Up Charges

It was still very early in the morning on Friday—probably before 5:00—when the Sanhedrin arrived at Pontius Pilate's place with Jesus in shackles. Remember, the Jewish leaders wanted this done as quickly as possible to avoid a public uproar. You can imagine Pilate wasn't too thrilled about "doing business" this early in the morning. And so his first words were basically, "All right, fellas . . . you better have a good reason for this. What's your accusation against this man?" (John 18:29). Their reply was deliberately evasive. They had actually convicted Jesus on charges of blasphemy, but they knew that wouldn't hold weight in getting Pilate to approve an execution. So "they answered and said to him, 'If He were not an evildoer, we would not have delivered Him up to you'" (John 18:30 NKJV).

The arrogance of their reply is astonishing. Basically, the Sanhedrin was demanding that Pilate take Jesus and execute Him without any questions asked. They pretended to be offended by Pilate's questioning of their integrity—as if they'd *ever* bring an innocent man to be executed.

Maybe it was too early for Pilate. Or maybe he just wanted to get rid of these pesky Jewish leaders who waltzed in before he'd had his coffee. Whatever the case, his response shows his indifference to the situation: "You take Him and judge Him according to your law" (John 18:31 NKJV). He was giving them approval to do with Jesus whatever their law demanded. Pilate probably assumed they'd eagerly accept his nod of approval and take Jesus out and stone Him. But he couldn't get rid of them that easily. They didn't want to stone Him themselves. (Notice how hypocritical they remained throughout this whole ordeal . . . they wanted Jesus killed, but they didn't want His blood on their own hands.)

No, the Sanhedrin wanted a Roman execution—the worst kind. Like Pilate, they were fearful of the people's opinions (Matt. 26:5). Turning Jesus over to the Romans made their plot so much more tidy. So they were determined to get Pilate to do the deed for them. They again lied to Pilate: "It is not lawful for us to put anyone to death" (John 18:31 NKJV).

10. Jesus had spoken before about His death—specifically about dying on a cross. By insisting on a Roman execution, what were the Sanhedrin doing, according to John 18:32?

_____

_____

_____

What had Jesus already told His disciples, according to Matthew 20:18–19?

_____

_____

_____

By now, Pilate had apparently woken up. Now he wanted more than a "he done it." If the Sanhedrin wanted him to execute Jesus, he needed more substantial charges against Him. The Jewish leaders knew they needed something that would cause this Roman official to justify an execution. They quickly fabricated new charges of sedition against Jesus. Luke writes, "They began to accuse Him, saying, 'We found this fellow perverting the nation, and forbidding to pay taxes to Caesar, saying that He Himself is Christ, a King'" (Luke 23:2 NKJV). In other words, they made Jesus out to be a revolutionary who had tried to persuade people into not paying Roman taxes and who had presented Himself as a king.

Pilate's Plan

Pilate wasn't dumb. He knew the Sanhedrin's charges against Jesus were iffy at best. He wanted the scoop up-close and personal. So he brought Jesus inside and questioned Him directly, hoping to get a better grasp on the facts and maybe understand why this Jesus posed such a threat to these Jewish leaders that they'd march Him over at 5:00 in the morning. What Pilate probably didn't expect was for Jesus to be so matter-of-fact about the situation. His answers were confident and straightforward: Yes, He was a king. But His kingdom, so He said, wasn't of this world.

What kind of answer was this? How was Pilate supposed to make a decision when this guy wasn't even making sense? Maybe this was a big deal to the religious leaders—but it was obvious Jesus' "kingdom" didn't pose an immediate threat to Rome.

Suddenly Pilate had an idea that could get both Jesus and these annoying priests to leave him alone. Jesus was from Galilee, a region under the authority of another

[Pilate] took water and washed his hands before the multitude, saying, "I am innocent of the blood of this just Person. You see to it."

—Matthew 27:24 NKJV

Roman official, Herod Antipas. Pilate figured he could hand this whole ordeal over to Herod, who was also in town for Passover season.

With Pilate's bidding, Jesus was taken to Herod's palace—a fairly short walk through the narrow city streets. By now, the city was awake. The movement of the military escort, the Sanhedrin, and the accumulating crowd would've drawn even more people to see what was going on. Word quickly began to spread through Jerusalem. Jesus was on trial.

> Whoever blasphemes the name of the LORD shall surely be put to death.
>
> —Leviticus 24:16 NKJV

The Freak Show

Herod wasn't interested in legal matters that morning. His only interest in Jesus was because he'd heard about the many miracles Christ had done throughout Galilee, and he wanted Jesus to perform one for him. He simply wanted some entertainment for the day. Herod was probably surprised at how different Jesus looked from the strong, prophetic miracle worker he expected to see. Jesus' face was already badly bruised and swollen from the abuse He had taken. Spit and blood were drying in His matted hair. Tired and physically weakened from a sleepless night, He stood before Herod, bound and under guard like a common criminal.

Most disappointing to Herod was Jesus' refusal to perform for him. Herod "questioned Him with many words, but He answered him nothing" (Luke 23:9 NKJV). After a while, Herod grew tired of questioning Jesus and decided to make sport of Him. "Then Herod, with his men of war, treated Him with contempt and mocked Him, arrayed Him in a gorgeous robe, and sent Him back to Pilate" (Luke 23:11 NKJV).

You can imagine Pilate's surprise and frustration when the Sanhedrin returned with Jesus and a larger-than-ever crowd of onlookers in tow. Things were quickly getting out of hand. Now it would be harder than ever for Pilate to end the matter without creating a scandal that might get back to Rome—or worse, starting a riot on the busiest day of the year in Jerusalem. Either way, Pilate's career could be jeopardized by this.

11. Pilate was more concerned about squelching a potential upheaval than dealing out justice. What does he offer to do in order to appease the crowds in Luke 23:13–16?

_____

_____

_____

DID YA KNOW?

Pilate actually proposed Jesus' release to fulfill a custom. As a diplomatic gesture toward the Jews, and to promote goodwill on the feast day, the Roman governor would release one Jewish prisoner from Roman custody every Passover. This was most likely a longstanding tradition that dated back even before Pilate's administration. Matthew says, "Now at the feast the governor was accustomed to releasing to the multitude one prisoner whom they wished" (27:15 NKJV). Matthew isn't suggesting that the Roman governor would automatically release whomever the people wished, allowing them to choose from all the prisoners in custody at the time. Instead, what he means is that a few offenders were selected by Roman officials and those names were given to the people as candidates from which to choose. Rome would grant an automatic pardon to the prisoner the people selected from the names proposed to them.

Last-Ditch Effort

Pilate decided to use the Passover custom of releasing one prisoner for his own benefit in a last-ditch effort to escape the dilemma the Sanhedrin had created for him. He gave the crowd an option of which prisoner to release. First there was Jesus, whose popularity among the common people was well-known. Less than a week before this, all Jerusalem turned out to welcome Jesus to the city and shout hosannas as He entered in a procession the people fashioned for Him.

Then there was Barabbas, a thug and repeat offender so foul that Pilate seemed sure the people would never choose him. This guy had been convicted of murder, sedition, and robbery (Luke 23:25; John 18:40). His crimes had made him infamous, and he was probably both hated and feared by the people. Pilate's plan would leave the people with no option but to choose Jesus' release over that of Barabbas. This way, Pilate could release Jesus, but rather than being seen as refusing to carry out the will of the Sanhedrin, he would be seen as obeying the will of the people. It was a brilliant diplomatic maneuver.

But it didn't work.

Word quickly began to spread through Jerusalem. Jesus was on trial.

A Harsh Request

Pilate posed the question one more time: "The governor answered and said to them, 'Which of the two do you want me to release to you?' They said, 'Barabbas!'" (Matt. 27:21 NKJV). The answer came back clearly and unanimously, without hesitation. Pilate was dumbfounded. He asked them, "'What then shall I do with Jesus who is called Christ?' They all said to him, 'Let Him be crucified!'" (Matt. 27:22 NKJV).

Pilate was still astounded. How could an entire mob have such strong feelings against a guy they had basically worshiped just a few days before? So he asked, "'Why, what evil has He done?' But they cried out all the more, saying, 'Let Him be crucified!'" (Matt. 27:23 NKJV). No matter what Pilate said, it was clear this bloodthirsty crowd would be satisfied with nothing less than Jesus' death.

12. Pilate had reached the end of his rope. He was finally out of options. What did Pilate do in order to demonstrate that he was acting under protest, according to Matthew 27:24?

_____

_____

_____

DID YA KNOW?

Pilate's ceremonial hand-washing was actually a Jewish ritual. Its meaning would've been familiar to the crowd. The Roman ruler was expressing contempt for the fact that they had railroaded him into becoming a part of the conspiracy against Jesus. He was giving them what they wanted, but he wanted to make it clear that he wasn't doing it willingly.

After the crowd's second request to have Jesus killed, Pilate sent Him off to be scourged. It's a segment of Christ's punishment hardly given airtime; Luke doesn't even mention it. And yet scourging was a punishment worse than being flogged or beaten, if you can imagine. Jesus, already exhausted, beaten, and bruised, now faced a scourging at the hands of sadistic, bloodthirsty Roman guards bent on bringing Him to the brink of death.

THAT'S GOTTA HURT

A Roman scourge was a short wooden handle with numerous long lashes of leather attached to it. Each leather strip had a sharp piece of glass, metal, bone, or other hard object attached to the end of it. The victim would be stripped of all clothing and tied to a post by his wrists, with his hands high enough over his head to virtually lift him off the ground. His feet would be dangling, and the skin on his back and buttocks completely taut. One or two scourge-bearers would then deliver blows, skillfully laying the lashes diagonally across the back and buttocks with extreme force. The skin would literally be torn away, and often muscles were deeply lacerated. It wasn't uncommon for the scourge-wounds to penetrate deep into the kidneys or lacerate arteries, causing wounds that in themselves proved fatal. Some victims died from extreme shock during the flogging.

The Final Decision

The apostle John records how after Jesus' scourging and the mockery that accompanied it, Pilate once more vainly tried to seek Jesus' release. He again brought Him before the crowd, this time dressed in a robe fashioned from a soldier's tunic, crowned with a crown of thorns, and "triumphantly" presented as a mock king. With Jesus probably unable to stand at this point, surely the crowd would be satisfied that He had suffered enough. But they weren't. "Therefore, when the chief priests and officers saw Him, they cried out, saying, 'Crucify Him, crucify Him!'" (John 19:6 NKJV).

Pilate, still astonished at the crowd's insatiable thirst for Jesus' blood, said to them, "You take Him and crucify Him, for I find no fault in Him" (John 19:6 NKJV). He'd had enough. He declared Jesus' innocence once more, verbally (and vainly) washing his hands of the matter.

13. Three times Pontius Pilate pronounced his assessment of Jesus. Each time, Christ's verdict was "not guilty." What were Pilate's words in each instance?

John 18:38 —

_____

_____

_____

Three times Pontius Pilate pronounced Jesus "not guilty."

John 19:4 —

_____

_____

_____

John 19:6 —

_____

_____

_____

14. What did the Jews threaten Pilate with in order to get their way, according to John 19:12?

_____

_____

_____

This was their trump card against Pilate. Their thinly veiled threat could've ultimately ended his career. He apparently recognized that and, feeling that he had no other choice, gave the order for Jesus to be crucified. He bartered away his eternal soul for temporary job security.

Remember that Jesus' trial had begun in the middle of the night based on nothing more than fabricated stories. Even after first coming to Pilate with insufficient evidence, Christ had been beaten to the brink of death and mocked as if He were the vilest of criminals. And now the highest ruler in the region had been utterly unable to stand in the way of the Crucifixion. There was no stopping it now.

Wrapping It Up

No one was permitted to speak in His defense. No voice of caution was raised at any point in the trial. No plea for mercy was entertained. None of the evidence that supported His claims was ever considered. Jesus was simply rushed through a kangaroo court into a guilty verdict that had been arranged and agreed upon long before He ever came to trial. Isaiah's prophecy, written at least seven hundred years earlier, perfectly described this moment: "He is despised and rejected by men, a Man of sorrows and acquainted with grief. And we hid, as it were, our faces from Him; He was despised, and we did not esteem Him" (Isa. 53:3 NKJV). Isaiah foretold the whole world's sinful apathy toward Jesus Christ. No one came to His defense. No one spoke in His favor. He was left to bear His affliction all alone.

Things to Remember

❧ The plan to do away with Christ wasn't just because the Jewish religious leaders hated His teachings; they were also scared of His increasing influence among the Jewish population.

❧ Jesus' trial was unjust and illegal by virtually every principle of jurisprudence known at the time.

❧ Many people came forward who were willing to bear false witness against Jesus, but none were found credible enough to sustain a charge against Him.

❧ Finally having accomplished the evil goal they had so long sought, the members of the Sanhedrin began to vent their hatred of Jesus openly.

❧ The Sanhedrin made Jesus out to be a revolutionary who had tried to persuade people into not paying Roman taxes and who had presented Himself as a king.

❧ Less than a week before this, all Jerusalem turned out to welcome Jesus to the city and shout hosannas as He entered in a procession the people fashioned for Him.

❧ It was clear that the bloodthirsty crowd would be satisfied with nothing less than the destruction of Jesus.

❧ Threatened by the Jewish crowd, Pilate felt he had no choice, so he gave the order for Jesus to be crucified.

Memorize This!

*"I have found no fault in this Man concerning those things of which
you accuse Him; no, neither did Herod, for I sent you back to him;
and indeed nothing deserving of death has been done by Him."*
—Luke 23:14–15 NKJV

Check This Out

If you want to find out more about the following related topics, check out John MacArthur's extensive resources in the *MacArthur LifeWorks Library CD-ROM*, or visit www.gty.org.

✠ The Sanhedrin
✠ Caiaphas and Annas
✠ Jewish legal procedures
✠ Bearing false witness
✠ Rome's role in Jerusalem
✠ Pontius Pilate
✠ Herod Antipas
✠ The zealots
✠ The fickle people

Notes

Lesson 7

A Cross to Bear

✠

And He, bearing His cross, went out to a place called the Place of a Skull, which is called in Hebrew, Golgotha, where they crucified Him, and two others with Him, one on either side, and Jesus in the center.
—John 19:17–18 NKJV

The Word to the Wise

Before starting this lesson, read Matthew 27:26–49.

For Starters

He could hardly open His eyes from the lack of sleep and repeated beatings. His senses reeled from the shock of pain from the brutal scourging He had endured. Staggering forward by sheer determination, Jesus continued on the path to the Cross. His face was raw where they had torn out His beard. Thorns pierced His scalp no matter which way He turned His head. Rough wood bit into His shoulder blades. All around Him was the sound of mockery, the slap of rough hands, the slime of spit hurled at Him. They heaped shame and disgrace on this self-proclaimed Messiah, but Jesus' agony had only just begun.

Verbal Lashes

The scourging ordered by Pilate was just the beginning of a long series of physical and emotional tortures Jesus endured. Next was the ferocious mockery from Roman soldiers, apparently handed out for their own kicks. These soldiers had no reason to heap such scorn on Jesus, yet they took great delight in giving it. They were hard men, a result of having witnessed numerous executions. The pain of torture no longer made any impact on them. As far as they were concerned, Jesus was just another religious fanatic with whom they were free to amuse themselves as cruelly as they pleased. This was a sick game for them.

Obviously, the Roman soldiers had no idea whom they were tormenting. To them, Jesus was just another criminal Pilate had ordered to scourge and crucify. But the cruel mockery they heaped on Him reveals their own wickedness. As they led Jesus back to the Praetorium, they deliberately made a spectacle of Him, much to the delight of the taunting crowd. The commotion drew the entire garrison of soldiers to watch.

> "I gave My back to those who struck Me, and My cheeks to those who plucked out the beard; I did not hide My face from shame and spitting."
>
> —Isaiah 50:6 NKJV

1. How do you think it's possible for these soldiers to have been so cruel? Why would they go out of their way to make a spectacle out of Jesus?

_____

_____

_____

2. Scripture plainly points to the wickedness of the human heart. Jesus' public humiliation put that wickedness on full display via the Roman soldiers. The cruelty they unleashed on Christ revealed the very sinfulness He was dying to forgive.

____ Genesis 6:5   a. Wash your heart from wickedness that you may be saved.

____ 1 Samuel 24:13   b. Those who follow wickedness are far from God's law.

____ Psalm 119:150   c. Wickedness proceeds from the wicked.

____ Proverbs 11:5   d. The wicked will fall by his own wickedness.

____ Jeremiah 4:14   e. The wickedness of man was great on the earth.

> "He who is hanged is accursed of God."
>
> —Deuteronomy 21:23 NKJV

A Roman cohort consisted of six hundred soldiers. These soldiers were stationed at the Antonio Fortress (which overlooked the temple mount from the north). They were an elite unit, assigned to serve the governor and to keep the fragile peace in this volatile region of the Roman Empire. Although Rome recruited soldiers from all its conquered regions, Jews were exempt from military service, meaning that all these soldiers would've been Gentiles. They were probably Syrian troops, because Syrians spoke Aramaic, and this would've been essential in Jerusalem. Some of these same soldiers were undoubtedly part of the group that had arrested Jesus in Gethsemane the previous night. Still, they probably had little knowledge of who He was. As far as they were concerned, He was just one in a long line of religious zealots who had troubled the peace and made problems for Rome. They undoubtedly assumed that He deserved whatever ridicule and torment they could heap on Him.

3. How does Isaiah 50:6 prophesy the Messiah will be treated?

_____

_____

_____

Condemned Roman prisoners were considered fair game for such abuse, as long as they weren't killed before the sentence of crucifixion could be carried out. The soldiers's abuse of Jesus wasn't motivated by any personal animosity toward Him, but it was still wicked to the extreme. The soldiers had become experts at such mockery, having overseen so many executions—but rarely did they have such enthusiastic crowds to play to. They evidently decided to make the most of it.

A Crown, a Robe, and a Scepter

Jesus had already been slapped and beaten repeatedly, even before He was delivered to Pilate, so His face was swollen and bleeding already. After the scourging, His back would be a mass of bleeding wounds and quivering muscles, and the robe they fashioned for Him would only add to the pain. Imagine rough cloth rubbing against raw, open flesh. They stripped Jesus of His own garments, which suggests He was literally naked apart from the robe they fashioned for Him.

Their goal was clearly to make a complete mockery of His claim that He was a king. To that end, they fashioned a crown of thorns. Caesar wore a laurel wreath as a crown; thorns were a cruel replica of that. These were no doubt the longest, sharpest thorns the soldiers could find; many varieties of these grow in Jerusalem to this day—some with two-inch barbed quills that would penetrate deep into His head as the crown was pressed hard upon Him. The reed in His hand was a further attempt to make fun of His royal claim. The reed represented a scepter, imitating the scepter Caesar carried on festive state occasions.

4. Though the soldiers were completely ignorant about who Jesus really was, their actions were significant in Jesus' eventual triumph. Check out how Scripture redeems this humiliating time of His life.

They placed a crown of thorns on Jesus' head, but how shall He be crowned according to Revelation 14:14?

_____

_____

_____

They threw a tattered robe around His shoulders, but what will be written on Jesus' robe, according to Revelation 19:16?

_____

_____

_____

They gave Him a reed for a scepter, but what does Psalm 45:6 say shall be placed in His hands?

_____

_____

_____

They thought He was nobody, but what will all of heaven and earth declare of Jesus, according to Revelation 5:13?

_____

_____

_____

Though the soldiers were completely ignorant about who Jesus really was, their actions were significant in Jesus' eventual triumph.

I am a worm, and no man; a reproach of men, and despised by the people.

—Psalm 22:6 NKJV

DID YA KNOW?

The robe was apparently made from an old tunic—probably an old garment that had been discarded by one of the soldiers. The Greek expression is *chlamus*, signifying a military cloak; not the same "gorgeous robe" used by Herod in Luke 23:11 (NKJV). Matthew says the robe was scarlet, but Mark 15:17 and John 19:2 call it "purple"—suggesting that it was a badly faded tunic. It was probably the nearest thing to purple (signifying royalty) the soldiers could find.

> All those who see Me ridicule Me; they shoot out the lip, they shake the head, saying, "He trusted in the LORD, let Him rescue Him."
>
> —Psalm 22:7–8 NKJV

Throughout it all, Jesus kept silent. His lack of words may have convinced the soldiers that He was a madman, and so they simply laid the mockery on thicker. Acting as if He were royalty, they bowed at His feet and condescendingly said, "Hail, King of the Jews!" Then, as the Jewish priests and bystanders had done, they spat on Him. One of the guards took the reed from His hand and used it to strike Him repeatedly on His head. The reed, though a flimsy scepter, would've been firm enough to inflict great pain on His already bruised head, while shoving the thorns deeper into His skull. The apostle John records that they also struck Him with their hands (John 19:3)—probably slapping with open hands while taunting Him some more. Most likely, the crowd was cheering them on as if they were watching a sport.

5. One day, according to Scripture, it will be God who mocks the wicked. How does Psalm 2:4–6 describe God's wrath?

_____

_____

_____

He who sits in the heavens shall _____;

The LORD shall _____ them in _____.

Then He shall _____ to them in His _____.

And _____ them in His deep _____:

"Yet I have set My _____ on My holy hill of _____"
(NKJV).

Public Humiliation

"And when they had mocked Him, they took the robe off Him, put His own clothes on Him, and led Him away to be crucified" (Matt. 27:31 NKJV). Victims of crucifixion were usually made to wear a sign around their necks on which was written the crime they were condemned for. It was part of the shame deliberately inflicted on those who faced crucifixion (Heb. 12:2; 13:13). To completely humiliate them, victims were led through the streets and made to walk in a public procession.

They were also forced to carry their own crosses to the place of execution. That practice was what Jesus referred to earlier in his ministry when He told the disciples, "Whoever desires to come after Me, let him deny himself, and take up his cross, and follow Me" (Mark 8:34 NKJV). A Roman cross large enough to crucify a grown man might weigh as much as two hundred pounds—an extremely heavy load to bear in any circumstances. But for someone in Jesus' weakened condition it would be virtually impossible to drag such a load from the Praetorium to a place of crucifixion outside the walls of Jerusalem.

6. Jesus stumbled under the weight of His cross, and the Roman soldiers grew impatient with His staggering. What did they do to remedy the situation, according to Matthew 27:32?

_____

_____

_____

Jesus' exhaustion is completely understandable. Remember that Jesus knew His time was nearing. It's possible He hadn't slept much that week, wrestling with the imminence of the task ahead. The previous day had been so grueling that His disciples had been unable to stay awake while He prayed in the Garden.

But that was only the beginning of agony for Jesus. He literally sweated blood in His intense grief and sorrow while He prayed. Then He was arrested, beaten repeatedly, held without sleep all night, beaten some more, scourged to the point of having His flesh shred, beaten, and mocked again. After several hours of such agony, combined with blood loss and shock, it's no wonder He was too weak to carry a two-hundred-pound cross to Calvary by Himself.

Just Passing By

Enter Simon. A foreigner from Cyrene, Simon wasn't an idle spectator joining the crowd to mock Jesus like everyone else. Mark 15:21 says, "He was coming out of the country and passing by" (NKJV). As Jesus was leaving the city, Simon was apparently entering, and by divine appointment, he was at exactly the right place at the right moment to be of help to Jesus.

Cyrene was an African city on the Mediterranean coast, in what is Libya today. A large Jewish community lived there, and Simon was probably a Jewish pilgrim who had made the long journey from Cyrene to Jerusalem for the Passover. Mark

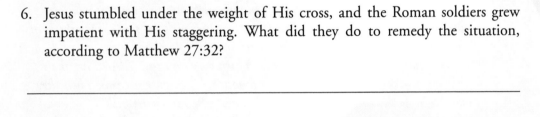

I looked for someone to take pity, but there was none; and for comforters, but I found none.

—Psalm 69:20 NKJV

identifies Simon as "the father of Alexander and Rufus" (Mark 15:21 NKJV). Mark was probably writing from Rome around AD 50, so Alexander and Rufus were most likely believers known to the church there. Paul sent greetings to "Rufus, chosen in the Lord, and his mother" in Romans 16:13 (NKJV). If it's the same Rufus, his mother would have been Simon's wife. It's not by chance that Simon is named in all three synoptic Gospels; his later history was obviously known to the Gospel writers, which undoubtedly means he later became a believer in Christ. Though he couldn't have been pleased about being forced to carry a condemned criminal's cross, it became a doorway to eternal life for him.

A Solemn Message

Believe it or not, in the midst of a physical breakdown, Jesus saw the opportunity to teach. In fact, His last public message was given on the road to Calvary. Luke describes it:

> And a great multitude of the people followed Him, and women who also mourned and lamented Him. But Jesus, turning to them, said, "Daughters of Jerusalem, do not weep for Me, but weep for yourselves and for your children. For indeed the days are coming in which they will say, 'Blessed are the barren, wombs that never bore, and breasts which never nursed!' Then they will begin 'to say to the mountains, "Fall on us!" and to the hills, "Cover us!"' For if they do these things in the green wood, what will be done in the dry?"
>
> —Luke 23:27–31 NKJV

Part of the message was a reference to Hosea 10:8—"They shall say to the mountains, 'Cover us!' and to the hills, 'Fall on us!'" (NKJV). It was a dire warning of disaster to come. Since in that culture childbearing was understood to be the highest blessing God could give a woman, only the worst kind of plague or disaster could ever cause anyone to say "Blessed are the barren, wombs that never bore, and breasts which never nursed!"

The green tree Jesus mentioned represented a time of abundance and blessing, and the dry tree stood for bad times. Jesus was saying that if a tragedy like this could happen in good times, what would befall the nation in bad times? If the Romans crucified someone whom they admitted was guilty of no offense, what would they do to the Jewish nation when they rebelled? Transcending time, Christ was referring to events that would happen less than a generation later, in AD 70, when the Roman army would lay siege to Jerusalem, utterly destroy the temple, and slaughter thousands upon thousands of Jewish people—multitudes of them by crucifixion.

They also gave me gall for my food, and for my thirst they gave me vinegar to drink.

—Psalm 69:21 NKJV

Believe it or not, in the midst of a physical breakdown, Jesus saw the opportunity to teach.

7. This wasn't the first bad message Jesus had given to Jerusalem. Jesus had spoken of the coming disaster in Luke 19:41–44 and had wept over it. What does that passage say would happen to the city?

_____

_____

_____

DID YA KNOW?

The Mosaic Law required that all executions occur outside the city walls (Num. 15:35; Heb. 13:12). But the Romans had a slightly different concept. They made sure that all crucifixions took place near a major intersection or road in order to make the condemned person a public example for everyone passing by. So Jesus' crucifixion took place outside the city, but in a heavily trafficked location carefully selected to make Him a public spectacle.

The Place of a Skull

The place where Jesus was crucified was called Calvary. The Aramaic name for it was Golgotha, meaning "a skull." Nowhere in Scripture is it called a hill, but it's generally assumed that this spoke of a craggy knoll or incline that looked like a skull. Today, just north of Jerusalem's city walls is a place known as Gordon's Calvary that can be seen and still bears an uncanny resemblance to a human skull.

Matthew writes, "And when they had come to a place called Golgotha, that is to say, Place of a Skull, they gave Him sour wine mingled with gall to drink. But when He had tasted it, He would not drink" (27:33–34 NKJV). Apparently just before they nailed Jesus to the cross, the soldiers offered Him this bitter drink. "Sour wine" is vinegar. "Gall" is something that tastes bitter. Mark 15:23 says the bitter substance was myrrh, which acts as a mild narcotic.

8. The vinegar and gall fulfilled a Messianic prophecy from Psalm 69:19–21. What words in this passage give us a picture of how Jesus was feeling at this time?

_____

_____

_____

> The place where Jesus was crucified was called Calvary. The Aramaic name for it was Golgotha, meaning "a skull."

> They divide My garments among them, and for My clothing they cast lots.
> —Psalm 22:18 NKJV

The soldiers may have offered it for its numbing effect just before they drove the nails through Jesus' flesh. When He tasted what it was, He spat it out. That seems like a natural, insignificant response, yet it's telling. Amazingly, Christ didn't want His senses numbed. He had come to the cross to be a sin-bearer, and He would feel the full effect of the sin He bore; He would endure the full measure of its pain. The Father had given Him a cup to drink more bitter than the gall of myrrh, but without the stupefying effect. At this point, any of us would've taken whatever we could—and as much of it as possible—to lessen the searing pain. But Jesus' heart was still steadfastly set on doing the will of the Father, and He wouldn't deaden His senses before He had accomplished all His work.

Excruciating Details

"Then they crucified Him" (Matt. 27:35 NKJV). The exact process used in Jesus' crucifixion is a matter of some speculation because none of the Gospel accounts gives a detailed description of the method used on Him. But we can glean a lot of information from the incidental details that *are* given. After the Crucifixion, the disciple Thomas remarks about Jesus' nail prints—"Unless I see in His hands the print of the nails, and put my finger into the print of the nails . . . I will not believe" (John 20:25 NKJV). From that, we can gather that Christ was nailed to the Cross rather than being tied to it by leather thongs, as was sometimes done. From Matthew 27:37, which states that His indictment was posted "over His head" (NKJV), we deduce that the form of cross He was nailed to was the familiar cross depicted today with the top of the upright protruding above the crossbar, rather than the often-used St. Anthony's Cross, a T-shaped stake.

We also can glean some of the details about how crucifixion victims died from secular accounts of crucifixion in Jesus' time. Christ would've been nailed to the cross as it lay flat on the ground. These nails were long, tapered iron spikes, similar to modern railroad spikes—but much sharper. They had to be driven through the wrists (not the palms of the hands), because neither the tendons nor the bone structure in the hands could support the body's weight. Nails in the palms would simply tear the flesh between the bones. Nails through the wrists would usually shatter carpal bones and tear the carpal ligaments, but the structure of the wrist was nonetheless strong enough to support the weight of the body. As the nail went into the wrist, it would usually cause severe damage to the nerves in the wrist, causing intense pain in both arms. Finally, a single nail would be driven through both feet, sometimes through the Achilles' tendons. Although none of the nail wounds would be fatal, they would all cause intense and increasing pain as the victim's time on the cross dragged on.

After the victim was nailed in place, several soldiers would slowly elevate the top of the cross and drop the foot into a deep posthole. The cross would land with a jarring blow into the bottom of the hole, causing the full weight of the victim to immediately fall on the nail-pierced wrists and feet. That would cause a bone-wrenching pain throughout the body, as major joints were suddenly twisted out of their natural positions.

> "If He is the King of Israel, let Him now come down from the cross, and we will believe Him."
>
> —Matthew 27:42 NKJV

9. That jarring blow is probably what David referred to prophetically in Psalm 22, a psalm about the Crucifixion. What does Psalm 22:14 say?

_____

_____

_____

If you're not already squeamish reading and imagining the details of Christ's crucifixion, think about this: the Romans had perfected the art of crucifixion in order to maximize the pain—and they knew exactly how to prolong the horror without permitting the victim to lapse into a state of unconsciousness that might relieve the pain. In other words, their methods ensured that the person would feel *every second* of his torture. The victim of crucifixion would experience waves of nausea, fever, intense thirst, constant cramps, and incessant, throbbing pain from all parts of the body. Sleeplessness, hunger, dehydration, and worsening infection all took their toll on the victim's body and spirit as the process of crucifixion dragged on—usually for three days or so. The feeling of utter hopelessness, the public shame, and the ever-increasing trauma to the body all intensified as the hours dragged on.

The emperor Tiberius is said to have preferred crucifixion as a method of punishment, precisely because it prolonged the victim's agony without granting relief by death. He believed death was an escape, so in his view execution wasn't really a punishment unless the victim had as much mortal agony inflicted as possible before death.

For those crucified, death normally came from slow suffocation. The victim's body would hang in such a way that the diaphragm was severely constricted. To exhale, he would have to push up with the feet so that the diaphragm would have room to move. Ultimately fatigue, intense pain, or muscle atrophy would leave the victim unable to do this, and he would finally die from the lack of oxygen.

Once strength or feeling in the legs was gone, the victim would be unable to push up in order to breathe, and death would occur quickly. That's why the Romans sometimes broke the victim's legs below the knees when they wanted to hasten the process (John 19:31).

Dehydration, shock, and congestive heart failure sometimes hastened death as well. In Jesus' case, it seems likely that acute exhaustion was probably another major contributing factor.

Stripped of All Dignity

Aside from the physical pain of crucifixion, the most notable feature of this type of execution was the stigma of disgrace attached to it. Victims were usually hanged naked. They were mercilessly taunted and reminded of the reason for their punishment. The whole point was to make a spectacle of shame and reproach out of them.

10. What was Jesus' opinion of the shame He faced on the cross, according to Hebrews 12:2?

_____

_____

_____

Scripture indicates that Christ was deliberately stripped of all clothing and dignity when He was crucified. In fact, the soldiers who kept guard over Him gambled for what remained of His clothing.

11. So many details of Christ's crucifixion were prophesied. Even this seemingly insignificant act was foretold.

Psalm 22:18 — "They _____ My _____ among them, and for My _____ they _____ _____" (NKJV).

Matthew 27:35–36 — "Then they _____ Him, and _____ His _____, casting lots, that it might be _____ which was spoken by the prophet: 'They _____ My _____ among them, and for My _____ they _____ _____.' Sitting down, they kept watch over Him there" (NKJV).

There may have been as many as five pieces of clothing for the soldiers to divide among themselves: sandals, a robelike garment, a headpiece, a belt, and a tunic. That was the traditional clothing for a Jewish man in Jesus' culture. Evidently the normal arrangement provided for the four guards charged with guarding a victim to distribute his clothing equally among themselves. If each selected one garment, a fifth garment would remain—which makes sense according to John's account: "The soldiers, when they had crucified Jesus, took His garments and made four parts, to each soldier a part, and also the tunic. Now the tunic was without seam, woven from the top in one piece. They said therefore among themselves, 'Let us not tear it, but cast lots for it, whose it shall be'" (John 19:23–24 NKJV). The tunic was a fine, woven outer garment that was seen as undoubtedly the best of all the garments. Because of that, it was the one they gambled for. After divvying up Jesus' garments, they sat down to keep watch over Him.

ANOTHER CONSPIRACY BLUNDER

Throughout the Crucifixion, God was sovereignly directing every incident. Step by step, every minute detail of Old Testament prophecy was fulfilled. But some people have argued that Jesus was simply a man who purposely engineered details of His life and death to coincide with selected Old Testament prophecies. They point to phrases such as "that the Scripture might be fulfilled" (John 19:28 NKJV) as proof that Jesus manipulated circumstances to give the appearance of fulfilling Scripture.

Think about it. How could one man guide the actions of the *thousands* of people who interacted with Him during His life? Even during Jesus' crucifixion, how would it be possible for a man who's hanging on a cross to *force* the Roman guards around Him to gamble for His clothes or give Him a drink of vinegar (these were two of the final prophecies Christ fulfilled)? Wow . . . you've probably heard some weak arguments, but that's about as weak as they come. —*The Gospel According to Jesus*

> "And they put up over His head the accusation written against Him: THIS IS JESUS THE KING OF THE JEWS."
>
> —Matt. 27:37 NKJV

A Sign of Truth

Pilate added to the mockery by having a large sign put over Jesus' head with the only actual indictment that had been brought against Him. "And they put up over His head the accusation written against Him: THIS IS JESUS THE KING OF THE JEWS" (Matt. 27:37 NKJV).

Each of the Gospel writers mentions the sign, but each gives a *slightly* different variation of what it said. Luke 23:38 and John 19:20 both say that the inscription was written in Greek, Latin, and Hebrew, so the variant readings are easily explained. Putting all the various accounts together, it appears the full inscription actually read, "THIS IS JESUS OF NAZARETH, THE KING OF THE JEWS."

12. The Sanhedrin complained about Pilate's placard. What did they quibble over, according to John 19:21, and what was Pilate's reply in verse 22?

_____

_____

_____

Two Thieves Join In

Christ was crucified between two thieves. As if He hadn't already received enough humiliation and persecution, even they decided to use their last breaths to mock Him. These were no petty purse-snatchers; the Greek term for "robbers" signifies that they were serious thugs who had existed as complete outlaws. It's possible they were Barabbas's accomplices, in which case Christ's cross was actually meant for their leader. Obviously, these weren't your average nice guys, since they used what little strength was available to them to taunt Christ, who had never done them harm. They mocked Him just for the sport of it, which speaks volumes about their true character.

13. The Sanhedrin. Roman soldiers. Bystanders. Thieves. Complete strangers. His own followers. It seems as if *everyone* joined in Jesus' humiliation of the Cross. Why do you think the heavenly Father allowed so many people to persecute His Son?

_____

_____

_____

14. The scene at the cross was foretold generations before Jesus' time. What does David prophetically describe in Psalm 22:6–8?

_____

_____

_____

I am a _____, and no _____;

A _____ of men, and _____ by the people.

All those who see Me _____ Me;

They _____ out the _____,

they _____ the _____, saying,

"He _____ in the LORD, let Him _____ Him;

Let Him _____ Him, since He _____ in Him!" (NKJV).

The Sanhedrin Gloat

Standing close to the entire scene were members of the Sanhedrin. They were no doubt gloating in Jesus' misery—possibly even inciting the crowds to mock Him. But the height of their hypocrisy was this: They had come to berate Jesus and witness the culmination of their evil plot before going home and sanctimoniously observing their Passover meals. They reveled in crucifying God, then went home to thank Him for His goodness.

Their mockery was a desperate attempt to convince themselves and all other witnesses that Jesus wasn't Israel's Messiah. It was impossible since, in their eyes, the Messiah couldn't be conquered. The fact that Jesus hung there dying so helplessly was proof, as far as they were concerned, that He wasn't who He claimed to be. So they reveled in their triumph, strutting and swaggering among the crowd of observers.

15. What was the taunt raised up by the men of the Sanhedrin, according to Matthew 27:42, 43? Don't these words sound strangely familiar?

_____

_____

_____

MISSING THE POINT

The scribes and chief priests who mocked Jesus while He was on the cross were the experts on God's Word. Originally, scribes functioned as transcribers of the Law and readers of the Scripture. They eventually became more like lawyers and religious scholars by interpreting both civil and religious law. The chief priests, who included the high priest and other priests, were also schooled in the Scriptures. But ironically, none of these guys realized that by mocking Jesus they were fulfilling Isaiah's prophecy regarding the Messiah: "He was despised and rejected by men, a Man of sorrows and acquainted with grief" (53:3 NKJV). They were sealing their own fate. —*The MacArthur Quick Reference Guide to the Bible*

Jesus endured that shame, that disgrace, and that pain for the joy set before Him—the redemption of His people.

They were the highest priests in Israel. They knew the Scriptures, yet their hearts made them blind to its words. They had everything to do with religion but nothing to do with God. They therefore bore the greatest guilt of all who participated in the humiliation of Christ. Although they pretended to sit in Moses' seat (Matt. 23:2), they didn't believe Moses (John 5:46). Although they claimed to be spokesmen for God, they were actually children of Satan (John 8:44).

Wrapping It Up

In those last hours Jesus suffered shame, disgrace, and pain. The crowds hurled pitiless taunting, shameless mockery, and wicked gloating as He hung on the Cross. And yet Jesus remained silent, never returning their insults. As the Son of God, He could have. He could've called on angels to sweep down, save Him, and destroy His mockers. Yet the only thing He had to say about His tormenters was in a tender plea to God for mercy on their behalf (Luke 23:34). And the only thing He had come to do—willingly, knowingly, and in submissive obedience to God—was to die. He knew something no one else on earth knew—that while the abuse and torture *men* heaped on Him were agony beyond our ability to fathom, it was nothing compared to the wrath of God against the sin He bore. He endured that shame, that disgrace, and that pain for the joy set before Him—the redemption of His people.

Things to Remember

- It seemed as if the whole world was against Jesus. Jews and Gentiles alike were now willfully, even gleefully, participating in His murder.
- The soldiers had become experts at mockery, having overseen many executions—but rarely did they have such enthusiastic crowds to play to.
- The soldiers' aim was clearly to make a complete mockery of Jesus' claim that He was a king.
- As Jesus was leaving the city, Simon was apparently entering, and by divine appointment, he was at exactly the right place at the right moment to be of help to Jesus.
- None of the nail wounds would be fatal, but they would all cause intense and increasing pain as the victim's time on the cross dragged on.
- The Romans had perfected the art of crucifixion in order to maximize the pain. Their methods ensured that the person would feel *every second* of his torture.
- Pilate added to the mockery by having a large placard put over Jesus' head with the only actual indictment that had been brought against Him.
- The Jews believed the Messiah couldn't be conquered. The fact that Jesus hung there dying so helplessly was proof, as far as they were concerned, that He wasn't who He claimed to be.

Memorize This!

Looking unto Jesus, the author and finisher of our faith, who for the joy that was set before Him endured the cross, despising the shame, and has sat down at the right hand of the throne of God.

—Hebrews 12:2 NKJV

Check This Out

If you want to find out more about the following related topics, check out John MacArthur's extensive resources in the *MacArthur LifeWorks Library CD-ROM*, or visit www.gty.org.

- ✠ Roman executions
- ✠ Crucifixion
- ✠ Messianic prophecies
- ✠ Suffering for your faith
- ✠ Hebrew burial practices

Notes

Lesson 8

Loving to the End

"Therefore My Father loves Me, because I lay down My life that I may take it again. No one takes it from Me, but I lay it down of Myself. I have power to lay it down, and I have power to take it again. This command I have received from My Father."

—John 10:17–18 NKJV

The Word to the Wise

Before starting this lesson, read Luke 23:39–46 and John 19:25–30.

For Starters

Jesus was completely exhausted and weak from blood loss. The rough wood rubbed against His raw skin, and His flesh ripped every time He mustered the strength to pull Himself up to breathe. The waves of searing pain and dizziness were overwhelming as His muscles cramped all over His beaten body. He was dying.

But Jesus still had something to say. Teeth clenched and barely clinging to consciousness, He was only able to speak with great difficulty in those final hours. And so He didn't waste His words.

The Last Words You'd Expect

Jesus' first words from the Cross could've been anything else. He could've asked His heavenly Father why . . . why did He have to endure so much? Or He could've put an end to the hatred and venom His scoffers continued to unleash on Him as He hung there. Just a few words would silence them—a loaded "You'll see" or a Schwartzenegger-ish "I'll be back" kind of thing.

Instead, the first words out of Jesus' mouth as He hung there were a plea for mercy on behalf of the very people who had done all this. Luke records that shortly after His cross was raised—while the soldiers were still gambling for His clothing—He prayed to God for forgiveness on their behalf: "And when they had come to the place called Calvary, there they crucified Him, and the criminals, one on the right hand and the other on the left. Then Jesus said, 'Father, forgive them, for they do not know what they do'" (23:33–4 NKJV). While others were mocking Him—just as the taunting and jeering got the loudest—Christ responded exactly how you or I would *not* have.

> And when they had come to the place called Calvary, there they crucified Him, and the criminals, one on the right hand and the other on the left. Then Jesus said, "Father, forgive them, for they do not know what they do."
>
> —Luke 23:33-4 NKJV

He could've threatened, lashed back, or cursed His enemies; instead, He prayed for them.

1. Have you ever prayed for your enemies? What did it take to get to that point?

_____

_____

_____

Why did Jesus spend His energy (and some of His last words) doing this?

_____

_____

_____

2. Scripture indicates that Jesus' prayers on our behalf didn't just end with His death or upon His return to heaven.

   In Romans 8:34, where does Paul say Christ is, and what is He doing?

_____

_____

_____

What does Hebrews 7:25 say about Jesus' current intercessory prayers?

_____

_____

_____

_____

> My God, My God, why have You forsaken Me? Why are You so far from helping Me, and from the words of My groaning?
>
> —Psalm 22:1 NKJV

> He poured out His soul unto death, and He was numbered with the transgressors.
>
> —Isaiah 53:12 NKJV

The whole meaning of the Cross is summed up in this one act of intercession: "For God did not send His Son into the world to condemn the world, but that the world through Him might be saved" (John 3:17 NKJV). Any mortal man, of course, would've wanted only to curse or insult his killers under these circumstances. What did it matter? They had already gotten their way? You might think Jesus, being God in the flesh, would want to call down a few thunderbolts from heaven to judge these wicked people around Him.

But Christ was on a mission of mercy. He was dying to purchase forgiveness for sins. And even at the very height of His agony, His heart was filled with compassion rather than hatred.

The phrase "for they do not know what they do" doesn't suggest that they were unaware that they were sinning. It's not as if the Sanhedrin, the Roman soldiers, or the mocking bystanders weren't coherent. Just because they were ignorant of the truth—that this *was* the Son of God—doesn't mean they weren't sinning. These people were behaving wickedly, and they knew it. Most were fully aware of their wrongdoing. Pilate himself had testified of Jesus' innocence. The Sanhedrin was fully aware that no legitimate charges could be brought against Him. The soldiers

and the crowd could easily see that a great injustice was being done, and yet they all willingly—and *happily*—participated. Many of the taunting spectators at Calvary had heard Christ teach and seen Him do miracles. They couldn't have really believed in their hearts that He deserved to die this way.

But they were ignorant of the enormity of their crime. They were blinded to the full reality that they were crucifying God the Son. They were spiritually insensitive because they loved darkness rather than light. As a result, they couldn't recognize that the One they were putting to death was the Light of the world.

3. In 1 Corinthians 2:8, how does Paul explain the actions of those who put Christ to death?

_____

_____

_____

Answered Prayer

Remember that throughout His life, Jesus' prayers were met with power. When He asked His Father for something, it came to be simply because He always walked in His Father's will. So how was this prayer from the cross answered? In innumerable ways . . . and fast. The first answer came with the conversion of one of the thieves on the cross next to Jesus (Luke 23:40–43). Another followed immediately, with the conversion of one of the soldiers who had crucified Christ (Luke 23:47). Other answers to the prayer came in the weeks and months that followed the Crucifixion—particularly at Pentecost—as untold numbers of people in Jerusalem were converted to Christ. No doubt many of them were the same people who had screamed for Jesus' death and railed at Him from the foot of the cross. We're told in Acts 6:7, for example, that a great number of the temple priests later confessed Jesus as Lord.

It's important to understand that Jesus' plea for His killers' forgiveness didn't guarantee the immediate and unconditional forgiveness of everyone who participated in the Crucifixion. Just because He said "Father, forgive them" didn't mean everyone would simply cruise into heaven. Just as when we intercede out of desperation for the soul of someone we know who is unsaved, Jesus was interceding on behalf of all who would repent and turn to Him as Lord and Savior. He was literally begging for His Father's mercy—on their behalf—because otherwise they would face God's wrath. Jesus' prayer was that when they finally realized the enormity of what they'd done and sought the heavenly Father's forgiveness for their sin, He would *somehow* look past their murdering of His beloved Son.

Divine forgiveness is never granted to people who remain in unbelief and sin. Those who clung to their hatred of Jesus were by no means automatically absolved from their crime by Jesus' prayer. But those who repented and sought forgiveness—like the centurion, or the thief on the cross, or the priests, or the people in the crowd—would find abundant mercy because of Christ's petition on their behalf.

But Christ was on a mission of mercy. He was dying to purchase forgiveness for sins. And even at the very height of His agony, His heart was filled with compassion rather than hatred.

4. We have a hard time forgiving someone who unintentionally hurt our feelings. How in the world could God so easily forgive those who murdered His Son?

_____

_____

_____

5. Mercy is one of the many attributes of God. Take a look at what each of these verses says about the great mercy of our Lord. Match them up with their references.

____	Nehemiah 9:17	a. Yes, our God is merciful.
____	Psalm 62:12	b. God, be merciful to me a sinner.
____	Psalm 116:5	c. You are God, gracious and merciful.
____	Joel 2:13	d. Jesus is a merciful High Priest.
____	Luke 18:13	e. To You, O Lord, belongs mercy.
____	Hebrews 2:17	f. Return to God, for He is gracious and merciful.

So why couldn't Jesus just think His prayer to the Father? After all, He was in constant communion with the Father. Why'd He bother expending all the energy it took to say these words out loud?

Again, it comes back to mercy. Jesus' prayer was a token of mercy offered to all who heard. He prayed aloud for their sakes (John 11:42). Their sin was so unfathomably heinous that if witnesses hadn't actually heard Him pray for His killers' forgiveness, most might have assumed they had committed an unpardonable offense.

6. We're offered forgiveness because of Christ's sacrifice on the cross. Even the men who put Him to death were offered forgiveness, on the spot. What does that say about God's character?

_____

_____

_____

According to Jeremiah 31:34, what happens when God forgives someone?

_____

_____

_____

God _is_ forgiveness. He created the whole concept because it's who He is. And Psalm 86:5 says the Lord is "ready to forgive" (NKJV). He wants every sinner, no matter how much or how badly they've spit in His face, to be reconciled to Him. For those who accept this win-win, no-strings-attached deal, He promises to lavish them freely with forgiveness. You may think you've been just as in-your-face with your wickedness as those who were part of Jesus' execution. Maybe it's hard for you to even think about

He bore the sin of many, and made intercession for the transgressors.

—Isaiah 53:12 NKJV

For God did not send His Son into the world to condemn the world, but that the world through Him might be saved.

—John 3:17 NKJV

things you've done in the past. *Whatever* the case, God still wants to forgive you and restore His relationship with you. Remember, it's who He is.

A Change of Heart

Here's a case in point. Remember the two thieves who hung beside Jesus? They'd both gone out of their way to hurl insults at Christ, even though He'd done nothing to them. Believe it or not, as the hours of agony passed on the cross, one of the two thieves had a change of heart. Scripture doesn't say what prompted the change. Perhaps the thief heard Jesus' prayer for mercy and was touched by it. Perhaps something clicked in his brain, and he realized that the prayer applied to him.

Whatever it was, the change was miraculous, because if you remember, this guy was undoubtedly the worst of the worst. He was scum. His whole life had been devoted to stealing things and making others' lives miserable. He chose to use the last of his dying strength to mock Christ—that's how bad he was. And yet suddenly he got it. He understood that Jesus was innocent. And so when his buddy started swearing at Jesus again, he perked up and said, "This Man has done nothing wrong" (Luke 23:41 NKJV).

Imagine the other thief's reaction. "Huh? Just a minute ago you were one-upping me on insults. Now you're *defending* this guy?" Obviously, the repentant thief had done some thinking. As he studied Jesus, suffering all that abuse so patiently—never reviling or insulting His tormentors—the thief began to see that this Man on the center cross was exactly who He claimed to be. The criminal's thoughts reached his heart, and his heart changed his words. And just like that, he went from insulting Jesus to praising Him.

7. Check out the exchange between the thief and Jesus.

    What was the repentant thief's rebuke in Luke 23:40–41?

    _____

    _____

    _____

    What did the repentant thief request from Jesus in Luke 23:42?

    _____

    _____

    What was Jesus' reply to the repentant thief in Luke 23:43?

    _____

    _____

    _____

God is forgiveness. He created the whole concept because it's who He is. And Psalm 86:5 (NKJV) says the Lord is "ready to forgive."

"A sword will pierce through your own soul."

—Luke 2:35 NKJV

The thief even won a prize as he hung there on his cross: Most Assured of a Place in Heaven. No one had ever received a more explicit assurance of salvation. This guy was given a blanket free pass into the Savior's kingdom. And it serves as one of the greatest biblical illustrations of justification by faith. This man had done nothing—absolutely *nothing*—to merit salvation. In fact, he'd spent his entire life directly opposing the principles of God's kingdom. At this point, he was in no position to do anything that would earn him an eternal spot with God. But realizing that he was in an utterly hopeless situation, the thief asked for only a modest token of mercy from Christ: "Remember me."

His request was a final, desperate, end-of-the-rope plea for a small mercy he knew he didn't deserve. It echoes the cry of the tax collector mentioned in Luke 18:13 who "would not so much as raise his eyes to heaven, but beat his breast, saying, 'God, be merciful to me a sinner!'" (NKJV). Obviously, for either guy to be given a freebie into God's kingdom, it had to be an act of God—and it was. In both cases, Jesus gave full and immediate assurance of complete forgiveness and eternal life. Both men stand as classic proof that justification is by faith alone.

8. Paul is pretty explicit when it comes to explaining that we are justified only by faith:

Romans 3:28 — "A man is _____ by _____ apart from the _____ of the _____" (NKJV).

Romans 5:1 — "Having been _____ by _____, we have _____ with God through our Lord Jesus Christ" (NKJV).

Galatians 2:16 — "A man is not _____ by the _____ of the law but by _____ in Jesus Christ" (NKJV).

Jesus' second set of words as He hung on the cross changed a thief's life for eternity. When the criminal asked Jesus to remember him, He didn't hesitate or say, "Um, I'll think about it" or even, "That depends on how you act for the remaining hours of your life." Nope, Jesus' answer sent a clear message to the thief: He was completely forgiven. He wasn't expected to atone for his own sins, do penance, or perform any ritual. Instead, his forgiveness was full, free, and immediate: "Today you will be with Me in Paradise."

That was all Christ said to him. But it was all the thief needed to hear. He was still suffering unspeakable physical torment, but the misery in his soul was now gone. For the first time in his life, he was free from the burden of his sin. The Savior right next to him was bearing that sin for him. Soon they would be in Paradise together. The thief had Christ's own word on it.

Greater love has no one than this, than to lay down one's life for his friends.

—John 15:13 NKJV

"We receive the due reward of our deeds; but this Man has done nothing wrong."

—Luke 23:41 NKJV

Caring for Mom

Jesus' enemies weren't the only spectators at the cross. As word got around Jerusalem that morning that Christ was under arrest and had been condemned to death by the Sanhedrin, some of His closest loved ones came to be near Him. John 19:25 describes the scene: "Now there stood by the cross of Jesus His mother, and His mother's sister, Mary the wife of Clopas, and Mary Magdalene" (NKJV). Some interpreters believe John mentions only three women, and that "His mother's sister" is the same person as "Mary the wife of Clopas." But that would mean these two sisters were both named Mary, which seems highly unlikely. Instead, it seems John was saying there were three women named Mary present (Jesus' mother, Mrs. Clopas, and Mary Magdalene), as well as a fourth woman (Mary's sister) whose name is not given—but it's possible she was Salome, the mother of James and John. John also indicates in verse 26 that he was present at the scene, referring to himself the way he did throughout his Gospel, as "the disciple whom [Jesus] loved" (John 21:20).

It's one thing to watch an acquaintance or a friend suffer through a death; it's another thing for a mom to watch her own son agonizing—on a cross, no less. Can you imagine what Mary (Jesus' mom) must have been thinking? She had reared Jesus from childhood. She knew better than anyone how perfect He was. And yet as she watched, crowds of people poured contempt on her Son, cruelly mocking and abusing Him. His bleeding, emaciated form hung helplessly on the cross, and all she could do was watch His agony. She couldn't reach up to wipe away the tears and the blood. She couldn't hold His hand or caress His head. She couldn't "fix" anything.

In the midst of His own pain, Jesus recognized His mom's suffering. And so He spoke for the third time from the cross: "When Jesus therefore saw His mother, and the disciple whom He loved standing by, He said to His mother, 'Woman, behold your son!' Then He said to the disciple, 'Behold your mother!' And from that hour that disciple took her to his own home" (John 19:26–27 NKJV). When Jesus said, "Behold your son," He wasn't referring to Himself. He probably nodded at John. He was delegating to John the responsibility to care for Mary in her old age. At his worst moment, He was still thinking of others—in this case, making sure His earthly mother was taken care of. It was a beautiful gesture, one that speaks volumes of the personal nature of Jesus' love. Although He was dying under the most excruciating kind of anguish, Jesus, the King of love, selflessly turned to care for the earthly needs of those who stood by His side.

> When Jesus therefore saw His mother, and the disciple whom He loved standing by, He said to His mother, "Woman, behold your son!" Then He said to the disciple, "Behold your mother!" And from that hour that disciple took her to his own home.
>
> —John 19:26–27 NKJV

DID YA KNOW?

Jesus addresses His mom as "woman." In fact, nowhere in the Gospels does He ever call her "mother"—only "woman." It wasn't a sign of disrespect. It simply underscored the fact that Christ was much more to Mary than a son. He was her Savior too. She wasn't some patron saint. She was as dependent on divine grace as the lowliest of sinners, and after Christ reached adulthood, her relationship to Him was the same as that of any obedient believer to the Lord. She was a disciple; He was the Master. Odd? Maybe. But what do you expect when she had changed God's diapers, only to have Him save her soul?

> "Lord, remember me when You come into Your kingdom."
>
> —Luke 23:42 NKJV

9. There were those who tried—and who still try—to elevate Mary's status because of her Son's greatness. What did one woman declare in Luke 11:27, and what in verse 28 did Jesus say in return?

_____

_____

_____

> A man is not justified by the works of the law but by faith in Jesus Christ.
>
> —Galatians 2:16 NKJV

It's interesting to note that Jesus didn't commit Mary to the care of His own half-brothers. Mary was evidently a widow by now. The Bible doesn't say a thing about Joseph after Jesus' birth and childhood. Apparently he had died by the time Jesus began His public ministry. But the Gospels clearly state that Jesus had brothers (Mark 3:31–35; John 2:12; Luke 8:19–21). Matthew even names them: "James, Joses, Simon, and Judas" (13:55 NKJV). Actually, they would've been half-brothers, as the natural offspring of Mary and Joseph.

So why didn't Jesus appoint one of His own brothers to look after Mary? The answer seems astounding. According to John 7:5, "His brothers did not believe in Him" (NKJV). Despite seeing Jesus' miracles up-close and personal, despite hearing His crazy teaching about God's kingdom and watching the consistency of His life, these guys still didn't believe their brother was who He said He was. Obviously, when you live with someone your whole life, you see the side of them others don't. You see their flaws and their weak spots. But Jesus didn't have any! He walked the walk and talked the talk.

It wasn't until Jesus rose from the dead that His brothers were finally convinced. Acts 1:14 records that they were among the group meeting for prayer in the Upper Room when the Holy Spirit came at Pentecost: "These all continued with one accord in prayer and supplication, with the women and Mary the mother of Jesus, _and with His brothers_" (NKJV, _emphasis added_). But they were evidently not believers yet when

Jesus died. So as He was dying on the Cross, He committed His mother to the care of His closest disciple, John.

Forsaken

Christ's fourth saying from the cross is by far the richest in mystery and meaning. Matthew writes, "Now from the sixth hour until the ninth hour there was darkness over all the land. And about the ninth hour Jesus cried out with a loud voice, saying, *'Eli, Eli, lama sabachthani?'* that is, 'My God, My God, why have You forsaken Me?'" (27:45–46 NKJV).

As Christ hung there, He was bearing the sins of the world. He was dying as a substitute for others, bearing the guilt of their sins, and suffering the punishment for those sins on their behalf. At the core of that punishment was God's wrath against sinners. Jesus wasn't just being beaten, crucified, and mocked by humans; He was facing the wrath of the Creator of the universe head-on. In some mysterious way during those awful hours on the cross, the Father poured out the full measure of His wrath against sin—only here, the twisted truth was that the recipient of that wrath was God's own beloved Son!

10. Why did Jesus get the brunt of God's wrath against sin if He was completely sinless?

_____

_____

_____

MORE THAN A BORE

We often say that Christ "bore our sins" on the Cross. But why? Where does that phrase come from? When the apostle Peter uses the word "bore" in 1 Peter 2:24, the term means "to carry a massive, heavy weight." And that's what sin is. It's so heavy that Romans 8:22 says, "The whole creation groans and labors" under its weight (NKJV). Only Jesus could remove such a weight from us. When Christ "bore our sins," He bore the penalty for our sins. He endured physical *and* spiritual death. When Jesus cried out on the Cross, "My God, My God, why have You forsaken Me?" (Matt. 27:46 NKJV), His was the cry of spiritual death. That was the penalty for bearing our sins.
—*Truth for Today*

"Now from the sixth hour until the ninth hour there was darkness over all the land. And about the ninth hour Jesus cried out with a loud voice, saying, 'Eli, Eli, lama sabachthani?' that is, 'My God, My God, why have You forsaken Me?'"

—Matt. 27:45-46 NKJV

And now we come to the true meaning of the Cross. This is the core, the entire reason Jesus went through all the literal hell that He did. Christ wasn't just giving us an example to follow. He wasn't just a martyr at the mercy of the wicked men who crucified Him. And He wasn't just making a public display so that people would see the awfulness of sin. In fact, He wasn't even offering a ransom price to Satan—or any of the other various explanations religious liberals, cultists, and pseudo-Christian religionists have tried to suggest over the years.

Here's what was happening on the cross: God was punishing His own Son as if He had committed every wicked deed done by every sinner who would ever believe. And He did it so that He could forgive and treat those redeemed ones as if they had lived Christ's perfect life of righteousness.

Did you catch that? *Really* catch that? God allowed all this to happen to Jesus so He could deal with us as if we'd never done *anything* wrong. Jesus gets crucifixion, while we get a free ride. It's almost incomprehensible why God would ever go through with such an unfair "deal."

> God allowed all this to happen to Jesus so He could deal with us as if we'd never done anything wrong.

11. Scripture frequently mentions this true meaning of Christ's death:

___	Isaiah 53:4–5	a. Messiah shall be cut off, but not for Himself.
___	Isaiah 53:9–10	b. Christ became a curse for us.
___	Daniel 9:26	c. He who knew no sin became sin for us.
___	Romans 8:3	d. Jesus Himself is the propitiation for our sins.
___	2 Corinthians 5:21	e. Jesus was wounded for our transgressions.
___	Galatians 3:13	f. Christ suffered once for sins to bring us to God.
___	1 Peter 3:18	g. Jesus' soul was made an offering for sin.
___	1 John 2:2	h. God sent His Son on account of sin.

You may have heard the word *propitiation* mentioned in church before. It's a big, fancy word that basically means an offering made to satisfy God. To remedy the stain of sin, God required a sacrifice—this was established when sin first entered the world through Adam and Eve. To remedy our sin situation, killing a perfect lamb—Christ—was the only solution. He was the only One who could satisfy God's requirement for sin. And because of God's awesome love, He offered His own Son as that sacrifice. In fact, "It *pleased* the LORD to bruise Him" (Isa. 53:10 NKJV, *emphasis added*). God the Father saw the travail of His Son's soul, and He was "satisfied" (Isa. 53:11 NKJV). Christ made propitiation by shedding His blood (Rom. 3:25; Heb. 2:17).

It was God's own wrath against sin, God's own righteousness, and God's own sense of justice that Christ satisfied on the cross. The shedding of His blood was a sin offering given to God. Christ died in our place—and He received the very same outpouring of divine wrath in all its fury that *we* deserved for our sin. It was a punishment so severe that any normal human could spend the rest of time in the torments of hell, and he still wouldn't have *begun* to exhaust the divine wrath that was heaped on Christ at the cross.

It can seem hard to grasp. It's certainly overwhelming. Yet *this* was the true measure of Christ's sufferings on the cross. The physical pains of crucifixion—horrific as they

were—were nothing compared to the wrath of the Father against Him. This was why He had looked ahead to the Cross with such horror, why He had sweat blood praying about it in the Garden. There's no way we can even begin to fathom all that was involved in paying the price of our sin. But it's safe to say that all our worst fears about the horrors of hell—and more—were realized by Him as He received the brunt of others' wrongdoing.

Worse yet, in that awful, sacred hour as He dealt with all this from the cross, it was as if the Father abandoned Him. Though there was surely no interruption in the Father's love for Him as a Son, God nonetheless turned away from Him and forsook Him as our Substitute. Why? Because our sin was so hideous God couldn't look at it; He couldn't be in its presence.

The fact that Christ—suffering from exhaustion, blood loss, asphyxia, and all the physical anguish of the Cross—nonetheless made this cry "with a loud voice" proves that He wasn't just reciting the words of Psalm 22:1 in order to fulfill yet another prophecy. This was coming from the depths of His soul. Every molecule of His being was crying out in anguish. And as we'll see in the following chapter, all nature groaned with Him.

Every molecule of His being was crying out in anguish.

Parched

"After this, Jesus, knowing that all things were now accomplished, that the Scripture might be fulfilled, said, 'I thirst!'" (John 19:28 NKJV). This was the fifth thing Christ said from the cross. As the end neared, Jesus finally asked for a tiny bit of physical relief. Earlier He had spat out the vinegar mixed with painkiller that the soldiers had offered. Now, when He asked for relief from being so dehydrated, He got nothing but a sponge saturated with pure vinegar. No one ran to get Him a Coke, or even a cup of water. John writes, "Now a vessel full of sour wine was sitting there; and they filled a sponge with sour wine, put it on hyssop, and put it to His mouth" (John 19:29 NKJV).

Remember, Jesus was truly human. His thirst, among other things, shows it. Sure, He was God incarnate; but in His physical body, He experienced all the normal human limitations of real human flesh. And none was more vivid than this moment of agonizing thirst after hours of hanging on the cross. He had suffered more in His body than few have ever suffered. Yet all He was given to salve His fiery thirst—again, so that the Scriptures might be fulfilled—was vinegar. "They also gave me gall for my food, and for my thirst they gave me vinegar to drink" (Ps. 69:21 NKJV).

12. Revelation 21:6 is reminiscent of Jesus' moment on the cross—only now, what does Jesus offer?

_____

_____

_____

Crying Victoriously

John's account of the Crucifixion continues: "So when Jesus had received the sour wine, He said, 'It is finished!'" (John 19:30 NKJV). In the Greek text, this sixth utterance of Jesus from the cross is a single word: *Tetelestai!* Luke 23:46 indicates He made this cry "with a loud voice" (NKJV).

In the movie *Braveheart*, William Wallace yells out at the moment before his death. It was a scream of freedom that simultaneously proclaimed his ultimate purpose and demoralized his enemies. Even through death, he won.

Jesus' cry here was infinitely more powerful. This was a cry of victory for all eternity. The cry to trump all cries. One that will echo throughout time. It was triumphant and full of rich meaning. He wasn't just yelling out of relief that His life was over. Jesus was declaring for all to hear that the work the Father had given Him to do was now complete. As He hung there, looking every bit like a pathetic, wasted victim, He nonetheless celebrated the greatest triumph in the history of the universe. Christ's atoning work was finished; redemption for sinners was complete; and He was triumphant.

Christ had fulfilled on behalf of sinners everything the Law of God required of them. Full atonement had been made. Everything the ceremonial law foreshadowed had been accomplished. God's justice was satisfied. The ransom for sin was paid in full. The wages of sin were settled forever. All that remained was for Christ to die so that He might rise again.

13. Jesus will forever be recognized and praised for His accomplishment on the cross. What is one of Jesus' titles, found in Hebrews 12:2?

_____

_____

_____

How does this relate to the Cross?

_____

_____

_____

> Christ had fulfilled on behalf of sinners everything the Law of God required of them. Full atonement had been made.

That's why it's impossible to add to the work of Christ for salvation. You can't add to His task by going through a religious ritual—baptism, penance, or anything else. You can't work harder or pray more fervently or say kinder things and inch your way past what He's done. Nothing more is required to be saved because Christ paid the price. *Tetelestai!* His atoning work is done. All of it. "For by grace you have been saved through faith, and that not of yourselves; it is the gift of God, not of works, lest anyone should boast" (Eph. 2:8–9 NKJV).

14. How do Christians sometimes try to add to their salvation? What kinds of things do we do to work our way into heaven?

_____

_____

_____

Why do you think believers fall into this trap?

_____

_____

_____

> And when Jesus had cried out with a loud voice, He said, "Father, into Your hands I commit My spirit." Having said this, He breathed His last.
>
> —Luke 23:46 NKJV

Still in Control

Christ's final saying from the cross, right after "It is finished!" was a prayer that expressed the absolute submission that had been in His heart from the very beginning. Luke records those final words: "And when Jesus had cried out with a loud voice, He said, 'Father, into Your hands I commit My spirit.'" Having said this, He breathed His last" (Luke 23:46 NKJV).

Christ died as no other man has ever died. In one sense He was murdered by the hands of wicked men (Acts 2:23). In another sense it was the Father who sent Him to the cross and bruised Him there, putting Him to grief—and it pleased the Father to do so (Isa. 53:10). Yet in still another sense, no one took Christ's life. He gave it up willingly for those whom He loved (John 10:17–18).

When He finally expired on the cross, it wasn't with a wrenching struggle against His killers. He wasn't caught off guard, neither was His life cut short by a single act of man. His final passage into death—like every other aspect of the Crucifixion drama—was a deliberate act of His own sovereign will, showing that to the very end, He was sovereignly in control of all that was happening. John says, "Bowing His head, He gave up His spirit" (19:30 NKJV). Quietly, submissively, He simply yielded up His life.

CAN'T TOP THAT

What would people think if you took a felt-tipped pen and tried to add more features to the Mona Lisa? What if you got a hammer and chisel and offered to refine Michelangelo's David? It would be a travesty. They're masterpieces! You can't add to them. In an infinitely greater way, the same is true of Jesus' atoning work. He paid the full price of our sins. He purchased our redemption. His offer of salvation from sin is complete in every sense. "It is finished!" Nothing we can do would in any way add to what He accomplished on our behalf. —*The Gospel According to Jesus*

Wrapping It Up

Christ was dead. To everyone who loved Jesus, His death on the cross seemed like the end of the world. Here was a guy who had said He was God's Son, which, to them, meant He would reign as victorious King of the world. This didn't seem too triumphant. They'd spent the last three years—some longer—watching and listening to this Man's every divine move. And this was it? This was the glorious ending?

We know that it wasn't. But to every person who witnessed that day, it was the end. Yet Jesus, His killers, the mocking crowd, Pilate, Herod, the Sanhedrin—everyone who played a part of the Crucifixion—had simply fulfilled their part in God's plan to the letter. Everything had come to pass exactly as prophecy said it would.

Still, the disciples felt as if every hope had been shattered. They were left with grief. Confusion. Sorrow. Shock. Doubt. What would they do now?

What they didn't realize was that this was the greatest moment of victory in the history of redemption. And Christ would make that fact gloriously clear when He burst triumphantly from the grave just days later.

Things to Remember

❧ Even at the very height of His agony, compassion was what filled Jesus' heart.

❧ As the hours of agony passed, one of the two thieves who had mocked Christ earlier had a change of heart.

❧ Even though He was in anguish, Jesus selflessly turned aside to care for the needs of those who stood by.

❧ The Father poured out the full measure of His wrath against sin, and the recipient of that wrath was His own beloved Son!

❧ God allowed all this to happen to Jesus so He could deal with us as if we'd never done *anything* wrong.

❧ As the end neared, Christ uttered a final plea for physical relief.

❧ Christ's atoning work was finished; redemption for sinners was complete; and He was triumphant.

❧ It seemed to all who loved Him like a supreme tragedy. But it was the greatest moment of victory in the history of redemption.

Memorize This!

Therefore He is also able to save to the uttermost those who come to God through Him, since He always lives to make intercession for them.

—Hebrews 7:25 NKJV

Check This Out

If you want to find out more about the following related topics, check out John MacArthur's extensive resources in the *MacArthur LifeWorks Library CD-ROM*, or visit www.gty.org.

✠ Justification by faith
✠ The last words of Jesus
✠ "Deathbed" salvation
✠ Forgiving our enemies
✠ Jesus' intercessory role
✠ Prayers of Jesus

Notes

Lesson 9

A Natural Response

"Truly this was the Son of God!"
—Matthew 27:54 NKJV

The Word to the Wise

Before starting this lesson, read Matthew 27:45–54.

For Starters

From the last lesson, we learned that Jesus' death on the cross wasn't just another gory Roman execution. This was God's true Lamb, dying to provide forgiveness for the sins of believers for all time. It was the greatest event in history . . . yet hardly anyone noticed. Jerusalem was jam-packed, as it was during most holidays. The roads were clogged with travelers coming and going as they prepared to celebrate the Passover. Aside from the festivities, it was an unremarkable time for most people. Then something happened that forced *everyone* to pay attention. Suddenly all nature seemed to respond to the sacrifice taking place. Christ's ordinary death quickly became extraordinary, as the accompanying supernatural phenomena proved.

Sky Turned Black

First came the darkening of the sky. Matthew writes, "Now from the sixth hour until the ninth hour there was darkness over all the land" (27:45 NKJV). Matthew was counting hours by the Jewish system, so the sixth hour would have been noon. It was the point in the day at which the sun should've been the brightest in the sky, and yet a darkness fell over all the land and remained for three hours.

This probably wasn't a total blackness, but rather a severe darkening of the normal daylight intensity of the sun. "Over all the land" is an expression that might refer to the land of Israel, or it could refer to the whole world. Seeing as this was the only Son of God—the Creator of all the universe—it makes sense to think that the sun itself was dimmed, so that the darkness would have been universal and not limited to the local area surrounding Jerusalem.

One thing we know for sure: This wasn't just a freak eclipse, because Passover always fell on a full moon. Obviously, a solar eclipse would be out of the question during the full moon. But as the Maker of the planets, God is certainly capable of doing some planetary light-tinkering. In fact, He'd done it before. During Moses'

> A day of darkness and gloominess, a day of clouds and thick darkness.
>
> —Joel 2:2 NKJV

time, darkness fell on Egypt because the plague of locusts was so thick that the flying insects blocked the sunlight (Ex. 10:14–15). In Joshua's time the opposite occurred, and the sun seemed to stand still over Israel for a whole twenty-four-hour period (Josh. 10:12–14). In Hezekiah's day, the shadows turned backward ten degrees as the earth's rotation seemed to reverse for about forty minutes (2 Kings 20:9–11).

1. Revelation 9:2 mentions the events of the Apocalypse, including where "the sun and the air were darkened" (NKJV). The darkening of the sun is commonly mentioned in Scripture as an apocalyptic sign. Check out these jaw-dropping prophecies.

   Isaiah 50:3 — "I _____ the _____ with _____, And I make _____ their covering" (NKJV).

   Joel 2:31 — "The _____ shall be turned into _____, and the _____ into _____, before the coming of the great and awesome day of the LORD" (NKJV).

   Amos 8:9 — "'And it shall come to pass in that day,' says the Lord GOD, 'that I will make the _____ _____ _____ at _____, and I will _____ the _____ in _____ _____'" (NKJV).

> The veil shall be a divider for you between the holy place and the Most Holy.
>
> —Exodus 26:33 NKJV

The sun going dark isn't just biblical folklore. According to some of the church fathers, the supernatural darkness that accompanied the Crucifixion was noticed throughout the world at the time. The historical writings of Roman-turned-Christian Tertullian that defended Christianity to pagan skeptics mention this event: "At the moment of Christ's death, the light departed from the sun, and the land was darkened at noonday, which wonder is related in your own annals and is preserved in your archives to this day."

2. Throughout Scripture, darkness is connected with judgment, and supernatural darkness of this type signifies cataclysmic doom. What words are used to describe the situation in each of these verses?

   Joel 2:2 —

   _____

   _____

   _____

Amos 5:20 —

_____

_____

_____

Zephaniah 1:14, 15—

_____

_____

_____

3. How were judgment and darkness related on the day of Christ's death?

_____

_____

_____

People have interpreted the darkness at the time of Jesus' death many different ways. Some suggest God sent it as a veil to cover the sufferings and nakedness of His Son, as an act of mercy toward Christ. Other people suggest the darkness signified His displeasure with those who put Christ to death. Scripture doesn't say why God made it dark; it only reports it as a fact.

It's safe to say the darkness does signify divine judgment. And because of that, it's possible that the darkness signified the Father's judgment falling on Christ as He bore in His person our guilt. Remember, all three Gospels that account for the darkness describe it as coming the last three hours of Jesus' life, when He was still alive. It could be that His suffering was the most intense during these hours that nature couldn't help but respond to His agony. Regardless of why it grew dark, we know that it was definitely the darkest time of Jesus' life, as proven by His heart-wrenching cry of "My God, My God, why have You forsaken Me?" (Matt. 27:46 NKJV).

The Veil Is Torn

The darkness came during Jesus' last few hours. But at the moment of His death, a series of remarkable miracles occurred. Matthew writes, "Then, behold, the veil of the temple was torn in two from top to bottom" (27:51 NKJV).

This veil wasn't a wimpy, sheer-fabric curtain for decoration. It wasn't just a makeshift shower curtain put up to section off part of the temple. This was a heavy-duty curtain that completely blocked the entrance to the Most Holy Place in the Jerusalem temple. It separated the public parts of the temple from the place where the ark of the covenant was kept. The ark symbolized the sacred presence of God, and He had designed this temple setup. In other words, it was a big deal, both physically and symbolically. Josephus described the veil as ornately decorated and made of blue woven fabric.

> Scripture doesn't say why God made it dark; it only reports it as a fact.

> Then, behold, the veil of the temple was torn in two from top to bottom.
>
> —Matt. 27:51 NKJV

4. The veil in the temple was modeled after the veil that had first hung in the tabernacle of Moses.

What did God tell His people that the veil should look like, according to Exodus 26:31?

_____

_____

_____

According to Exodus 26:33 and Hebrews 9:3, what purpose did the veil serve?

_____

_____

_____

Jesus' sacrifice tore the veil so that believers could have what, according to Hebrews 6:19?

_____

_____

_____

> He guards all his bones; not one of them is broken.
>
> —Psalm 34:20 NKJV

> The veil was of vital symbolic importance, signifying "that the way into the Holiest of All was not yet made manifest."
>
> —Heb. 9:8 NKJV

Only one person went behind the veil: the high priest. And He wasn't back there watching football and enjoying some nachos with God every Sunday afternoon. The high priest entered the Most Holy Place only once a year, on the Day of Atonement, with the blood of a sacrifice. The veil was of vital symbolic importance, signifying "that the way into the Holiest of All was not yet made manifest" (Heb. 9:8 NKJV). In other words, it was a constant reminder that because of our sinfulness, humans were unfit for the presence of God. The fact that the sin offering was offered annually—and countless other sacrifices repeated daily—showed that sin was a big deal. It couldn't just be erased by making a simple animal sacrifice.

5. God required sacrifice, yet Psalm 40:6 says, "Sacrifice and offering You did not desire" (NKJV). Hebrews 10:4 lays on the reality even thicker: "For it is not possible that the blood of bulls and goats could take away sins" (NKJV). So why do you think God still wanted His people to offer sacrifices?

_____

_____

_____

6. Hebrews expresses the part Jesus plays on our behalf. Take a look at Hebrews 9:11–12.

   What role does Jesus fulfill?

   _____

   _____

   _____

   What blood did He bring into the Most Holy Place?

   _____

   _____

   _____

   The High Priest of Israel had to do this annually. How often does Jesus have to make this sacrifice?

   _____

   _____

   _____

   What did Jesus obtain for us by doing this?

   _____

   _____

   _____

> They made His grave with the wicked—but with the rich at His death, because He had done no violence, nor was any deceit in His mouth.
>
> —Isaiah 53:9 NKJV

The tearing of the curtain at the moment of Jesus' death dramatically symbolized that His sacrifice was a sufficient atonement for sins forever. The way into the Most Holy Place was now open. In other words, the entire Levitical system of rituals, animal sacrifices—even the priesthood itself—was done away in the moment of His death. The redeemed now had free and direct access to the throne of grace without the need for priest or ritual (Heb. 4:16).

But notice that the veil was torn from top to bottom. This was—and still is—hugely significant. It was impossible for any human to do this. God Himself had to remove the barrier. The tearing of the high curtain was basically God declaring, "My Son has removed this veil and eliminated the need for it through a single, perfect, once-for-all sacrifice that cleanses the redeemed from their sins forever. The way into My holy presence is now open to every believer, and the access is free and unobstructed."

> The tearing of the curtain at the moment of Jesus' death dramatically symbolized that His sacrifice was a sufficient atonement for sins forever.

7. Christ's passion and death made it possible for us to come before God.

How does Hebrews 4:16 say we can now come before God's throne?

_____

_____

_____

Those who reject Jesus will suffer what consequence, according to 2 Thessalonians 1:9?

_____

_____

_____

> Christ's passion and death made it possible for us to come before God.

> Now in the place where He was crucified there was a garden, and in the garden a new tomb in which no one had yet been laid.
>
> —John 19:41 NKJV

It was the Friday of Passover when Jesus died. That means that when the tearing of the veil occurred, the temple was packed with worshipers who were there for the killing of their Passover lambs. By God's design, it was in the very hour that those thousands of lambs were being slain that the true Passover Lamb died. Jesus wasn't just a symbol for those lambs; He was the real deal. He perfectly fulfilled all the symbolism of the worship in the temple. From that day on, all the temple ceremonies lost their significance, because what they were meant to foreshadow had finally arrived.

It would be another forty years before the temple itself would be completely destroyed when Titus sacked Jerusalem. But the true end of the Old Testament sacrificial system didn't occur with the destruction of the temple in AD 70. Remember all the Sanhedrin hoopla over Christ's words that He would destroy and rebuild the temple (John 2:19–22)? Here it was. The true end of the temple system occurred at the moment of Jesus' death, when God sovereignly declared His Son's passing a sufficient sacrifice for sins forever. The result was a supernatural splitting of the temple veil from top to bottom that opened the way into His presence.

Not Just a Slight Shake

Darkness and a torn temple veil weren't the only miracles surrounding Christ's death. At the exact moment Jesus died, Scripture says "the earth quaked, and the rocks were split" (Matt. 27:51 NKJV). If you've ever lived through a major earthquake, you know it's an extremely frightening ordeal. We're not talking a little shake here and there. If rocks were splitting at the time of Jesus' death, it's safe to say this was no little shimmy. An earthquake powerful enough to split rocks would be a *significant* tremor. (The crowd in the temple probably assumed the earthquake was the cause of the tearing of the veil.) Such a powerful quake would be a terrifying experience for everyone in the region of Judea. Although earthquakes were a fairly common phenomenon, an earthquake with enough force to split rocks would have instantly brought the entire city of Jerusalem to a halt for several minutes.

8. As with darkness, earthquakes in Scripture often signify a graphic display of divine judgment. In particular, they signify God's wrath. Match up these illustrations of the earth shaking and quaking before God's great wrath.

___ Exodus 19:18	a.	Sinai moved because of the presence of God.
___ 2 Samuel 22:8	b.	The mountains quake, the hills melt, the earth heaves.
___ Psalm 18:7	c.	God's voice shakes the earth.
___ Psalm 68:8	d.	The earth shook and trembled because God was angry.
___ Isaiah 24:19	e.	The foundations of the hills also quaked and were shaken.
___ Nahum 1:3–5	f.	When Moses met with God, the mountain quaked.
___ Hebrews 12:26–27	g.	Every mountain and island will be moved out of place.
___ Revelation 6:14–15	h.	The earth is violently broken, split open, and shaking.

A supernatural earthquake like this one was a sure sign of God's wrath. At the Cross, the wrath of God against sin was poured out on His own Son. The accompanying earthquake, coming at the culminating moment of Christ's atoning work, was a kind of divine punctuation mark, perhaps signifying God's anger at the fact that sin had cost His Son so much.

That's Just Crazy!

Now we get to the good stuff. As if the sky going black wasn't enough. As if earthquakes and symbolic temple-trashing wasn't enough. Now God has to go and do the truly unbelievable. Check out what else happened the moment Christ died: "The graves were opened; and many bodies of the saints who had fallen asleep were raised; and coming out of the graves after His resurrection, they went into the holy city and appeared to many" (Matt. 27:52–53 NKJV).

Many of the tombs in and around Jerusalem to this day are hollow stone sepulchers, resting at ground level or just above. The earthquake was evidently powerful enough to split sepulchers like these. But that wasn't the miracle; that could've occurred in any major earthquake. The great miracle is that those who were dead began walking out of these tombs.

Let's pause for a second and think about this. Jesus had raised people from the dead before. His episode with Lazarus is certainly one of the most renowned, although it wasn't the only time Jesus brought someone back to life. But here we don't even have Jesus laying hands on anyone or telling anyone to "Come forth!" (John 11:43 NKJV). Jesus isn't even on the scene anymore, so to speak . . . He's dead! And yet what does His death bring? New life! The power of His sacrifice *immediately* had results—to the very second.

Of all the Gospel writers, only Matthew mentions this event. Some critics have said this is why Matthew's account shouldn't be considered true. They reason that if such an event occurred, it would've certainly been noteworthy enough to catch the

"I lay down My life that I may take it again. No one takes it from Me, but I lay it down of Myself."

—John 10:17–18 NKJV

attention of all Jerusalem. But what makes them think this miracle was designed to capture people's attention? Despite its spectacular nature, it seems to have been a remarkably quiet miracle. Maybe it was intended this way.

Although "many . . . saints who had fallen asleep" were raised, not all were. These were select representatives of the multitude of believers buried in and around Jerusalem. The number raised isn't specified, but the term "many" in this case could refer to as few as a dozen—or even fewer. (That would still be "many," given the fact that what Matthew is describing is people who were released from stone sarcophaguses and came alive!) Still, despite the spectacular nature of the miracle itself, this seems to have been a fairly low-key event.

Notice, in fact, that those who rose from the dead didn't appear in Jerusalem until after Jesus' Resurrection. So where did all these ex-mummies go for the weekend? We don't know. Maybe they stayed at the closest Holiday Inn. Scripture doesn't say. But the fact that they waited until after Christ's Resurrection to appear to anyone reminds us that, as it says in 1 Corinthians 15:20, He is the firstfruits of those risen from the dead.

And it gets better. These risen believers most likely came forth from the dead in "glorified" bodies already fit for heaven (rather than being restored to life in regular, mortal bodies, as Lazarus had been). In other words, they may have looked completely different, since they were basically walking around in their heavenly forms. We know they "appeared to many" (Matt. 27:53 NKJV). Can you imagine how freaked out you'd be if you saw someone on earth in his other heavenly "skin"?

Again, how many they appeared to isn't specified, but evidently there were enough eyewitnesses to verify the miracle. When Matthew wrote his Gospel, some of the eyewitnesses would've still been alive. Matthew doesn't say what became of the risen saints, but they undoubtedly ascended to glory not long after Jesus' Resurrection.

Their appearance proved that Christ had conquered death, not merely for Himself, but for all the believers (we're considered saints). One day "*all* who are in the graves will hear His voice and come forth" (John 5:28–29 NKJV, *emphasis added*). This miraculous event foreshadowed that final great resurrection found in the End Times.

9. These resurrections were just the tip of the iceberg of the miracles to come.

   According to Romans 6:4, in what way will we follow where Christ has led?

   _____

   _____

   _____

   What will be given to those who have the Spirit dwelling in them, according to Romans 8:11?

   _____

   _____

   _____

He glorified God, saying, "Certainly this was a righteous Man!"

—Luke 23:47 NKJV

All who are in the graves will hear His voice and come forth.

—John 5:28–29 NKJV

What does Paul say will happen to us at Christ's return, according to 1 Corinthians 15:52?

_____

_____

_____

Change of Heart

Supernatural, unbelievable miracles are great. But perhaps the most important miracle that occurred at the moment of Jesus' death was the conversion of the centurion charged with overseeing the Crucifixion. The story quickly turns from the impossible to the touching. As Christ's atoning work was brought to completion, its dramatic saving power was already at work in the lives of those who were physically closest to Him. Matthew 27:54 says, "So when the centurion and those with him, who were guarding Jesus, saw the earthquake and the things that had happened, they feared greatly, saying, 'Truly this was the Son of God!'" (NKJV).

DID YA KNOW?

A Roman centurion was the commander of a hundred-man division (or a "century")—the basic building block of a Roman legion. There were about twenty-five legions in the entire Roman army worldwide. Each legion comprised six thousand men, divided into ten cohorts of six hundred men each. Each cohort had three maniples, and each maniple was divided into two centuries. Each century was commanded by a centurion. The centurions were usually career officers, hardened men of war.

Because this particular officer was with those guarding Jesus, it's very likely that he was in charge of overseeing and carrying out the crucifixion of Christ—and probably the crucifixions of the two thieves as well. He and his men were close eyewitnesses to everything that had happened since Jesus was taken to the Praetorium. They had personally kept Him under guard from that point on. (It's even possible that the centurion and some of the men with him were also the same soldiers who arrested Jesus the night before. If so, they had been eyewitnesses from the very beginning of the entire ordeal.)

Matthew 27:54 (NKJV) says, "So when the centurion and those with him, who were guarding Jesus, saw the earthquake and the things that had happened, they feared greatly, saying, 'Truly this was the Son of God!'"

10. The Roman centurion had watched the entire drama of the passion unfold. He had taken an active part in the brutal proceedings. Take a few minutes to consider just what this man had seen and done. Then jot down what event each of these verses references.

Mark 14:45 —

_____

_____

_____

Luke 22:51 —

_____

_____

_____

Mark 14:56 —

_____

_____

_____

Matthew 26:67 —

_____

_____

_____

Luke 23:4 —

_____

_____

_____

Mark 14:61 —

_____

_____

_____

John 19:2 —

_____

_____

_____

Then, behold, the veil of the temple was torn in two from top to bottom.

—Matthew 27:51 NKJV

John 19:1 —

_____

_____

_____

John 19:17 —

_____

_____

_____

Mark 15:25 —

_____

_____

_____

John 19:19 —

_____

_____

_____

Luke 23:34 —

_____

_____

_____

Matthew 27:56 —

_____

_____

_____

John 19:24 —

_____

_____

_____

Luke 23:43 —

_____

_____

_____

Luke 23:45 —

_____

_____

_____

Matthew 27:54 —

_____

_____

_____

> "When the centurion, who stood opposite Him, saw that He cried out like this and breathed His last, he said, 'Truly this Man was the Son of God!'"
>
> —Mark 15:39 NKJV

These soldiers had seen how Jesus held His silence while His enemies hurled accusations and insults at Him. They had strapped Him to a post for the scourging, and watched while He suffered even that horrific beating with quiet grace and majesty. They themselves had mercilessly taunted Him, dressing Him in a faded soldier's tunic, pretending it was a royal robe. They had battered His head with a reed they gave Him as a mock scepter. These same officers had also woven a crown of massive thorns and mashed it into the skin of His scalp. They had spat on Him and taunted Him and mistreated Him in every conceivable fashion—and they had seen Him endure all those tortures without cursing or threatening any of His tormentors.

In all likelihood, the soldiers heard with their own ears when Pilate repeatedly declared Jesus' innocence. They knew full well that He wasn't guilty, and that He didn't pose the slightest threat to Rome. From the very beginning, they must've been amazed about how different He was from the typical criminal who was crucified—though they obviously wouldn't reveal their astonishment. They had been inclined to write Him off as a madman. But by now they could see that He wasn't insane. In fact, He really wasn't like *any* of the hundreds of misfits they had crucified before. This guy was certainly different.

Until now, the uniqueness of Christ had made no apparent impact whatsoever on these soldiers. They were hardened men, and Jesus' passivity made no difference in the way they treated Him. Maybe they just thought He was a wimp or a mute. His obvious innocence hadn't gained any sympathy from them. They had showed Him no mercy. They were professional soldiers, trained to follow orders. And so they had dutifully nailed Jesus' hands and feet to the cross. They had set the cross upright and dropped it into the hole dug for it. They had cast lots for Jesus' garments. And then they had sat down to watch Him die. They were simply doing their job.

But they also heard Jesus pray for His killers. They saw the noble way He suffered. They heard when He cried out to His Father. They experienced three full hours of supernatural darkness. And when that darkness was followed by an earthquake at the

exact moment of Christ's death, it became pretty tough to ignore the fact that this guy really was the Son of God.

Mark suggests that there was something about the way Jesus cried out that struck the centurion as supernatural—maybe because of the powerful volume coming from someone in such a weakened condition. Mark writes, "When the centurion, who stood opposite Him, saw that He cried out like this and breathed His last, he said, 'Truly this Man was the Son of God!'" (15:39 NKJV).

An Immediate Effect

Apparently, it was the earthquake that sealed the deal for the centurion. "When [they] saw the earthquake and the things that had happened, they feared greatly" (Matt. 27:54 NKJV). Notice that Matthew indicates all the soldiers had the same reaction. When the earthquake occurred, they "feared greatly." It's a phrase that, in the original Greek, speaks of extreme alarm. It's exactly the same expression Matthew used to recount how Peter, James, and John reacted on the Mount of Transfiguration when Christ's glory was unveiled (Matt. 17:6). It's also the same kind of fear that was typical when people suddenly realized the truth about who Jesus was (Mark 4:41).

When the soldiers around the Cross heard Jesus' exclamation, saw Him die, and then immediately felt the earthquake, reality hit. It suddenly became all too clear to them that they had crucified the Son of God. They were stricken with terror. It wasn't just the earthquake that they were afraid of. They were terrified by the sudden realization that Jesus was innocent—and not merely innocent, but He was who He said He was. God's blood was literally on their hands. The centurion remembered the indictment of the Sanhedrin ("He made Himself the Son of God," John 19:7 NKJV), and having witnessed Jesus' death up close from beginning to end, he gave his own verdict on the matter: "Truly this was the Son of God!"

His words were straight from the heart. And just like that, his faith was changed for good. Luke says, "He *glorified God*, saying, 'Certainly this was a righteous Man!'" (23:47 NKJV, *emphasis added*). So the centurion—and according to Matthew, the soldiers with him—were evidently the very first converts to Christ after His Crucifixion, coming to faith at precisely the moment He expired.

Keeping Up Appearances

The Sanhedrin had already been "inconvenienced" enough by this Jesus fiasco. As soon as He was dead, they wanted His body taken down from the cross so it wouldn't stay there overnight and defile the Sabbath (remember, their Sabbath was actually Saturday). This upcoming Sabbath was an important day for them because, as the Sabbath following Passover, it was considered part of the Feast of Unleavened Bread. But isn't it ironic how sacred they treated the Sabbath in light of what they had just done to the Lord of the Sabbath Himself (Mark 2:28)? It's yet another indication of how they were completely into keeping up appearances rather than actual matters of faith.

When the soldiers around the Cross heard Jesus' exclamation, saw Him die, and then immediately felt the earthquake, reality hit. It suddenly became all too clear to them that they had crucified the Son of God. They were stricken with terror.

DID YA KNOW?

Old Testament law (Deut. 21:23) strictly commanded that the body of anyone hanged on a tree be removed and buried out of sight, not left hanging all night. But it's almost certain that most victims of Roman crucifixion were left hanging on crosses for days. Because this was Passover, and an especially high Sabbath at that, the Sanhedrin wanted the Jewish law observed. That's why they petitioned Pilate not to permit the bodies to remain on the crosses overnight.

11. Jesus always saved His harshest words for hypocrites—something the Sanhedrin certainly were. In Matthew 23:14, what does Jesus say would eventually happen to this pretentious group?

_____

_____

_____

The Sanhedrin wanted Jesus dead—as quickly as possible. So they asked for His legs to be broken. It wasn't an unusual request during a crucifixion. The breaking of the legs would make it certain that death would occur almost immediately, because once the legs could no longer push up to support the body's weight, the diaphragm would be severely constricted, and air couldn't be expelled. The victim would die of asphyxiation within minutes. But it was also a viciously cruel practice. It virtually guaranteed that the victim would die in as much pain as possible (as if being crucified was enough).

Pilate's soldiers came to the crucifixion site at the Sanhedrin's request. The legs of both criminals were broken. Within minutes, the forgiven thief was in Paradise with the Lord, who had preceded him to glory.

But the soldiers, finding Jesus already dead, decided not to break His bones.

12. Even the soldiers' failure to break His legs was a further fulfillment of Old Testament prophecy. What was foretold in Psalm 34:20?

"He _____ all his _____; not _____ of them is _____" (NKJV).

13. The soldiers didn't break Jesus' legs because they were pretty sure He was already dead. What did one of the men do, just to be certain, according to John 19:34?

_____

_____

_____

YEAH, RIGHT

Some people dispute the resurrection of Christ from the dead by saying that He never died but only fainted. Supposedly He was revived by the coolness of His tomb, got up, and walked out. Let's think about that case. First, the Roman executioners made sure He was dead. After breaking the legs of the thieves crucified alongside Him to speed up their deaths, the soldiers discovered that Jesus had already died. Second, they verified His death by piercing His side, out of which came a flow of blood and water. If Jesus had been alive, only blood, not water, would've come out (John 19:31–37). And third . . . how in the world can you explain Him moving the big stone blocking His tomb all by Himself? Christ was as dead as dead can be. And that means His Resurrection was real. — *Truth for Today*

Controlled Time

Mark 15:43–44 says that after Jesus' death, Joseph of Arimathea came to ask Pilate for the body of Jesus, and "Pilate marveled that He was already dead; and summoning the centurion, he asked him if He had been dead for some time" (NKJV). For those familiar with death by crucifixion, Jesus' early death wasn't normal. Crucifixion was designed to maximize the victim's pain while prolonging the process of dying. Victims sometimes suffered as long as four days before dying. Yet Jesus died after only a few hours.

It certainly wasn't that Jesus was a wimp (as if you could call anyone enduring crucifixion a "wimp"). Rather, it's further proof that throughout the entire process, Jesus was in complete control. What He had told the Jewish leaders was now true: "Therefore My Father loves Me, because I lay down My Life that I might take it again. No one takes it from Me, but I lay it down of Myself. I have power to lay it down, and I have power to take it again. This command I have received from My Father" (John 10:17–18 NKJV). Christ was even sovereign over the timing of His own death.

"Therefore My Father loves Me, because I lay down My life that I might take it again. No one takes it from Me, but I lay it down of Myself. I have power to lay it down, and I have power to take it again. This command I have received from My Father."

—John 10:17–18 NKJV

14. When the Roman soldiers were done with Him, Jesus' friends were allowed to step in and prepare His body for burial.

What did Joseph of Arimathea ask Pilate for, as recorded in Mark 15:43?

_____

_____

_____

According to John 19:39, what did Nicodemus provide for the burial of Jesus?

_____

_____

_____

How did Nicodemus and Joseph of Arimathea prepare Jesus' body for burial, according to John 19:40?

_____

_____

_____

What did Joseph of Arimathea offer for Jesus' use, according to Matthew 27:59–60?

_____

_____

_____

Everyone loves a happy ending. In fact, sometimes all we care about is the ending.

Wrapping It Up

Everyone loves a happy ending. In fact, sometimes all we care about is the ending. We fast-forward through a recorded TV show just to find out how an episode ended. We peek at the back of the book before reading it all just because we want to know the story's conclusion. In the same way, many people fast-forward through Jesus' Crucifixion to get to the Resurrection. After all, *that's* the Good News, isn't it?

Not entirely. Of course, the greatest news ever told is that Christ is alive and well today, that He endured the cross and yet still lives. But it's important—no, it's *essential*—for us to understand that without the Cross, there would be no Resurrection. For believers, the Good News isn't just that Christ became victorious by overcoming death; it's that He was sacrificed *in our place*. Because of His suffering on the cross, we have an open-door policy with God. We can enjoy and enter His presence freely, not simply because Jesus lives, but because He paid the price for our sin.

That's why the early church focused as much on the death of Christ as on His Resurrection. Paul wrote, "We preach Christ crucified" (1 Cor. 1:23 NKJV); "I

determined not to know anything among you except Jesus Christ and Him crucified" (2:2 NKJV); and, "God forbid that I should boast except in the cross of our Lord Jesus Christ" (Gal. 6:14 NKJV). And it's why "Jesus Christ and Him crucified" remains the very heart and soul of the gospel message. Without the atoning work Christ did on the cross, His Resurrection would be a wonder for us to stand back and admire. But it would have no personal ramifications for us. Instead, "if we died with Christ,"—that is, if He died in our place—then "we believe that we shall also live with Him" (Rom. 6:8 NKJV). *That's* the Good News!

Things to Remember

- At the moment the noon sun should have been brightest in the sky, darkness fell over all the land and remained for three hours.
- The veil was a constant reminder that because of our sinfulness, humans were unfit for the presence of God.
- The tearing of the high curtain from top to bottom proved that it was God Himself who removed the barrier.
- An accompanying earthquake, coming at the culminating moment of Christ's atoning work, was a kind of divine punctuation mark.
- The earthquake was powerful enough to split tombs, and those who emerged from them were raised from the dead.
- Perhaps the most important miracle that occurred at the moment of Jesus' death was the conversion of the centurion charged with overseeing the Crucifixion.
- At the very moment of Christ's death, the soldiers could no longer ignore the fact that Christ was indeed the Son of God.
- Having witnessed Jesus' death up close from beginning to end, the centurion rendered his own verdict on the matter: "Truly this was the Son of God!"
- After finding Jesus already dead, the soldiers decided not to break His legs.
- Christ was dead, but death hadn't conquered Him.
- Don't ever pass over the meaning of the death of Christ on your way to celebrate the Resurrection.

Memorize This!

Therefore we were buried with Him through baptism into death,
that just as Christ was raised from the dead by the glory of the
Father, even so we also should walk in newness of life.
—Romans 6:4 NKJV

Check This Out

If you want to find out more about the following related topics, check out John MacArthur's extensive resources in the *MacArthur LifeWorks Library CD-ROM*, or visit www.gty.org.

- ✠ The veil in the temple
- ✠ Earthquakes
- ✠ God's wrath against sin
- ✠ Centurion's salvation
- ✠ Jewish burial customs
- ✠ Joseph of Arimathea
- ✠ Nicodemus

Lesson 10

An Amazing Ending

✠

"He is not here; for He is risen, as He said."
—Matthew 28:6 NKJV

The Word to the Wise

Before starting this lesson, read Matthew 28:1–10 and John 20:1–18.

For Starters

The disciples had scattered, fear and despair clouding their minds. What was happening? How could Jesus be dead? How could everything end so quickly? Would the Sanhedrin or the Romans come after them next? By all accounts, the "bad guys" had won. They had captured Jesus, accused Him, and sentenced Him to a horrible death. He had suffered agony and shame, dying in public disgrace. His lifeless body had been removed to a cold tomb. And now a solid rock, an official seal, and an armed guard stood between them and the Teacher they had believed in. It seemed like the end of everything. Over. Finite. Or was it?

What they didn't know was the deeper meaning of why Jesus had died. What they didn't understand was God's sovereign plan that had a different ending. And death having the last word wasn't part of it.

Body Check

"Now after the Sabbath, as the first day of the week began to dawn, Mary Magdalene and the other Mary came to see the tomb" (Matt. 28:1 NKJV). John specifically mentions that these women made their way to the tomb "while it was still dark" (John 20:1 NKJV). The Sabbath had ended at sundown on the previous evening, and this was the dawning of Sunday, the first day of the week. When the Jews made reference to dates and times, they included any portion of a day as a day. Christ had been crucified on Friday and died before sunset, which marked the beginning of the Sabbath. He had remained buried all day Saturday. And the women arrived at the tomb on Sunday morning. So when calculating the number of days that had passed since Jesus had died, this Sunday was the third day.

Did they remember Jesus' words about rising again? Or were they simply curious since no one else had been able to get close to the tomb? Whatever their reason, it's

> On the third day He will raise us up, that we may live in His sight.
>
> —Hosea 6:2 NKJV

obvious they'd been thinking about it all weekend, because they took the first chance they got to go to the tomb.

1. The Lord had repeatedly taught that His Resurrection would be on the third day.

   Matthew 16:21 — "From that time Jesus began to _____ to His _____ that He must go to Jerusalem, and _____ many things from the elders and chief priests and scribes, and be _____, and be _____ the _____ _____" (NKJV).

   Matthew 17:23 — "They will _____ Him, and the _____ _____ He will be _____ _____. And they were exceedingly _____" (NKJV).

   Mark 10:34 — "They will _____ Him, and _____ Him, and _____ on Him, and _____ Him. And the _____ _____ He will _____ _____" (NKJV).

   Luke 18:33 — "They will _____ Him and _____ Him. And the _____ _____ He will _____ _____" (NKJV).

✠

DID YA KNOW?

"The first day of the week" (Matt. 28:1 NKJV) can also be translated as an interesting Greek phrase that literally means, "day one with reference to the Sabbath." The Jews didn't have names for days of the week, such as Monday, Tuesday, and so on, but simply numbered them in relation to the Sabbath. Sabbath means "seventh," referring to the seventh day of creation, when God rested. Although it was at the end of the week, because it was the central and holy day, all other days were based upon it—as the first, second, third, and so forth, day after the Sabbath.

They will kill Him, and the third day He will be raised up.

—Matthew 17:23 NKJV

Their reason for going may have involved a bit of curiosity, but it was also medical. In those days, dead bodies were prepared and wrapped with spices and ointments. In the predawn light, Mary Magdalene and the other Mary came to the grave with a small portion of sweet-smelling spices. Although they'd probably been on hand when Joseph of Arimathea and Nicodemus had wrapped Jesus' body in linens and spices (Matt. 27:61), they personally wanted to anoint their Lord (Luke 24:1).

2. Matthew focuses in on the two Marys—Mary Magdalene and Mary, the mother of James and Joseph (Mrs. Clopas)—but there were actually four women at the tomb that morning. List the other two mentioned in Mark 16:1, Matthew 27:56, and Luke 24:10.

_____

_____

_____

Undoubtedly, these women expected to find Jesus wrapped in His grave cloths and lying in the tomb. Why else would they have brought additional spices? All four of these women deeply loved Jesus. They had ministered to Him while He preached in Galilee. They had stood with Him while He hung on the cross (Matt. 27:55–56). Now, they had come to look at the grave. Perhaps they hoped the Roman soldiers would move the massive stone for them so that they could minister to Jesus one last time. Most likely, they simply wanted to do something more for Jesus' burial, which had been conducted in such a hurry two days earlier.

3. Mary had hoped to anoint Jesus for His burial. But what had Jesus already revealed about His anointing in Matthew 26:6–13?

_____

_____

_____

> "They have taken away the Lord out of the tomb, and we do not know where they have laid Him."
> —John 20:2 NKJV

Sure, these women missed Jesus' point about rising from the dead. After all, *everyone* had. But give them credit. Their love and devotion for Christ remained steady. They had shown the courage needed to attend Jesus' Crucifixion, and they had gathered at the first opportunity to plead with the Romans for the chance to see Him again.

Rolling Stone

They had one problem—a *big* problem. The stone in front of the tomb's door was huge. It wasn't a one-woman job, or even a four-woman job. In fact, it had required several strong men to ease the stone into place. So as they traveled along the way to Jesus' tomb, the women discussed among themselves, "Who will roll away the stone from the door of the tomb for us?" (Mark 16:3 NKJV). They knew they couldn't budge it by themselves. But just as they entered the garden, and Christ's tomb came into view, they saw that the stone had already been rolled away from the entrance. The tomb was open.

"And behold, there was a great earthquake; for an angel of the Lord descended from heaven, and came and rolled back the stone from the door, and sat on it" (Matt. 28:2 NKJV). Apparently, when the angel had descended, it had caused the earth surrounding Jesus' tomb to tremble violently. This was the second supernaturally caused earthquake in connection with Jesus' death and burial, the first one having occurred at the moment of His death (Matt. 27:51). The angel had been sent to open the grave, and none of Rome's safeguards could keep him back. The guards dropped into a stupor, the seal was broken, and the heavy stone was whisked aside in an instant.

But the angel didn't roll away the stone so Jesus could come out. Jesus was already risen and had left the tomb. The angel was sent so that the women and the disciples could get in. It was that important for them to see for themselves that the tomb lay empty.

> "Go quickly and tell His disciples that He is risen from the dead."
>
> —Matthew 28:7 NKJV

4. It seems that Mary Magdalene rushed out of the garden as soon as she "saw that the stone had been taken away from the tomb" (John 20:1 NKJV). What did she assume had happened, according to John 20:2?

_____

_____

_____

Unfortunately, Mary Magdalene missed the angel's announcement of Jesus' Resurrection. As soon as she saw the empty tomb, her heart sank, and her first response was to run and get help. She hurried to break the awful news to Peter and John. Like all of Jesus' followers, it never occurred to her that Jesus might have been resurrected. So she naturally assumed someone had broken in and stolen Jesus' body. Obviously, Peter and James didn't consider resurrection as an option either. So they ran all the way to the tomb to find out what had happened (John 20:3–4).

Freak Out

Talk about freaky. The tomb was glowing. It was an unbelievable sight. The angel who had rolled the stone aside looked like lightning, and his shining garment was as white as snow.

5. Angels aren't fairy-tale beings. They're found throughout the Bible, and are often described in frightening terms.

How is one of the heavenly creatures described in Ezekiel 1:14?

_____

_____

_____

How does Daniel describe the one in his vision in Daniel 10:6?

_____

_____

_____

What was the angel who appeared to Cornelius in Acts 10:30 wearing?

_____

_____

_____

How are the angels in Revelation 15:6 arrayed?

_____

_____

_____

The guards were petrified by the angelic visitor. Their trembling was so violent that they shook with fear. In the Greek, "shook" has the same root as "earthquake." In other words, the Roman soldiers on guard at the sealed entrance to the tomb experienced a personal earthquake when the angel arrived. But it didn't last long. Within moments, the soldiers became like dead men, fainting away with paralyzing fear.

The women also became frightened at the sight of the bright angel, but unlike the guards, they were reassured by God's messenger.

6. Every time men and women were confronted with the startling appearance of the supernatural in the Bible, their first response was fear. And right on cue, the angels' first words were "Fear not!" or "Do not be afraid!"

> I will turn their mourning to joy.
>
> —Jeremiah 31:13 NKJV

Daniel 10:12 — "Do not _____, Daniel, for from the first day that you set your heart to _____, and to _____ yourself before your God, your words were _____; and I have _____ because of your words" (NKJV).

Luke 1:13 — "Do not be _____, Zacharias, for your _____ is _____" (NKJV).

Luke 1:30 — "Then the angel said to her, 'Do not be _____, Mary, for you have _____ _____ with God" (NKJV).

Luke 2:10 — "Then the angel said to them, 'Do not be _____, for behold, I bring you _____ _____ of _____ _____ which will be to all people'" (NKJV).

Revelation 1:17 — "When I saw Him, I fell at His feet as dead. But He _____ His _____ _____ on me, saying to me, 'Do not be _____; I am the First and the Last'" (NKJV).

The angel knew the routine. Humans are frail; they get scared easily. It was important to reassure these women they didn't have to be scared. "Fear not" (Matt. 28:5 KJV). Since the angel's appearance had already frozen the soldiers with fear, his words to the women were intended to ease their minds. These women had simply come to the tomb out of their great love for Jesus. And now the angel had been sent to bring these women words of comfort, assurance, and love: "I know that you seek Jesus who was crucified. He is not here; for He is risen, as He said" (Matt. 28:5–6 NKJV).

Say What?

This didn't make sense. Of course, nothing seemed to make sense right now, seeing as there was a glowing being (apparently from heaven) sitting on the huge rock that could only be moved by several muscle men, telling them not to worry—this after scaring the Roman soldiers out of their wits.

The angel understood their frazzled state. And so he offered them proof. "Come, see the place where the Lord lay" (Matt. 28:6 NKJV). He invited the women to see the empty tomb for themselves. Inside, he had to reiterate his message just to wake them out of their disbelief: "Do not be alarmed. You seek Jesus of Nazareth, who was crucified. He is risen! He is not here" (Mark 16:6 NKJV). The angel's words were slowly beginning to sink in. Obviously, these women were having trouble accepting everything they saw and heard. There were the burial cloths, just where they'd been when Joseph of Arimathea and Nicodemus had finished with their preparations.

Just a little while later, Peter and John would enter this same space, and they'd see "the linen cloths lying there, and the handkerchief that had been around His head, not lying with the linen cloths, but folded together in a place by itself" (John 20:6–7 NKJV). Jesus hadn't needed to be unwrapped from the grave cloths that enveloped His body any more than He had needed to have the stone removed to leave the tomb. One moment He was encased in linen, and the next He was free.

The women stood stunned inside the tomb. While they looked around, a second angel joined them. Together, the angels gave the women still another reminder. "Why do you seek the living among the dead? He is not here, but is risen! Remember

Behold, I am alive forevermore.

—Revelation 1:18 NKJV

how He spoke to you when He was still in Galilee, saying 'The Son of Man must be delivered into the hands of sinful men, and be crucified, and the third day rise again'" (Luke 24:5–7 NKJV). For the third time, these women had the truth of Jesus' Resurrection repeated to them.

7. If Jesus had told His followers about His imminent Resurrection so often before, why do you think these women had such a hard time coming to grips with the scene?

_____

_____

_____

DID YA KNOW?

When the second angel joined the first inside the tomb, they seated themselves on the place where Jesus had been laid out. "One at the head and the other at the feet" (John 20:12 NKJV). Their positions are reminiscent of the two golden cherubim, positioned on either side of the mercy seat on the ark of the covenant (Ex. 25:18). Only now the angels were posted on either side of the place where Jesus had been the One who had just sacrificed His own life and became the means for every person to find mercy from God.

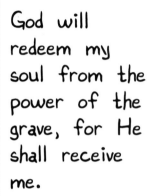

> God will redeem my soul from the power of the grave, for He shall receive me.
>
> —Psalm 49:15 NKJV

A Personal Visit

The angels didn't stop with this message of good news. It wasn't enough for these women to know that Jesus was risen. Others had to know, and so the angels next said, "Go quickly and tell His disciples that He is risen from the dead" (Matt. 28:7 NKJV). They did as they were told, and "went out quickly from the tomb with fear and great joy" (Matt. 28:8 NKJV). The appearance of angels had shaken them, despite the words of assurance. But fear was tempered now by joy, and the incredible hope that Jesus was indeed risen.

Meanwhile, Mary Magdalene had missed the whole scene. At the first signs of interference at the tomb, she'd turned back to report the discovery to the disciples. After telling Peter and John, they had all raced back to the tomb, where they discovered the linen burial cloths lying empty. By this time, the other women and the angels had all left the garden, and the two men, disappointed and confused, "went away again to their own homes" (John 20:10 NKJV). So Mary was left alone in the garden.

It must have been a lonely moment for Mary. Jesus had meant more than anything to her. He was the One who had given her a new life, saving her from her lifestyle of prostitution and showering her with undeserved love. Now He was gone, and things just seemed too overwhelming for her with an empty tomb, a rolled-away stone, and no explanations. So she stayed outside the tomb and began to weep in the garden.

The Lord must have been deeply touched, because she was the first to see Him in His resurrected state. First, two angels appeared to her inside the tomb as she peered in. They asked her why she was crying. After explaining to them what she thought had happened, another voice asked her the same question. Only this time, it was Jesus Himself. At first, she didn't recognize Him, mistaking Him for the gardener. But when Jesus called Mary by her name, she knew Him for who He was. "Rabboni!" (John 20:16 NKJV).

All it took was a single personal touch from Jesus, and Mary instantly recognized her Savior. He called her by name, probably in a way that was more intimate than anyone ever had before. And she knew exactly who was speaking.

Like the other women, Mary brought the good news to the other disciples in Jerusalem (John 20:18). Jesus was alive, and she had seen Him, and spoken with Him, and touched Him! And the disciples believed her, celebrated with her, and everyone lived happily ever after, right?

Not so fast. After all they'd been through, the disciples were a little too down in the dumps to believe stories about ghosts walking around town. All this "Jesus is alive" talk seemed like a tease. As her way of coping with grief, Mary surely was imagining things. They weren't about to believe a story *that* far-fetched (Mark 16:11).

> Those who sleep in the dust of the earth shall awake.
>
> —Daniel 12:2 NKJV

The Right Response

Meanwhile, the other women were making their way to Jerusalem to report their discovery to the disciples as well. "And as they went to tell His disciples, behold, Jesus met them" (Matt. 28:9 NKJV). The wording in this verse suggests that Jesus greeted these women in a very ordinary way. Here was the glorified Christ, having just conquered death and sin, nodding and saying "Good Morning" as He met the women hurrying toward Him along the road. It was as casual as a "Whazzup?" or a "Hey!" exchanged as you pass your friend in the school hallway.

It may have been an ordinary greeting, but the women nonetheless immediately recognized Jesus. Their response was a blend of awe and worship. "So they came and held Him by the feet and worshiped Him" (Matt. 28:9 NKJV). There wasn't doubt in their minds now. Jesus was truly the risen Messiah. He was Christ, the Son of God. As they stood in His presence, their only response was to praise and adore Him.

8. Confronted with the glorified Christ, these women threw themselves at His feet to worship Him. What does Philippians 2:10–11 say that all people will do when Jesus returns?

_____

_____

_____

9. Why, then, is worship such an important part of our lives?

_____

_____

_____

Making an Entrance

Earlier in the week, before Jesus was crucified, He had told His disciples, "But after I have been raised, I will go before you to Galilee" (Matt. 26:32 NKJV). This message was reiterated by the angel at the tomb, who told the women, "He is going before you into Galilee; there you will see Him" (Matt. 28:7 NKJV). After He was raised, Jesus confirmed His instructions, telling the women, "Go and tell My brethren to go to Galilee, and there they will see Me" (Matt. 28:10 NKJV).

But technically Jesus didn't appear to the disciples first in Galilee. He actually came to them on several occasions before meeting them there. He appeared first to Peter (Luke 24:34). He met two disciples on the road to Emmaus (Luke 24:15). On the evening of Resurrection Sunday, He met the ten disciples that were assembled (John 20:19), and eight days later to all eleven, after Thomas had joined them (John 20:26). But Jesus' words were still true. He hadn't broken His promise. He was merely setting the stage for His grand entrance in the strategic place of Galilee. There "He was seen by over five hundred brethren at once" (1 Cor. 15:6 NKJV), and it was there that the eleven disciples were commissioned to their apostolic ministry.

DID YA KNOW?

Galilee was a region to the north of Jerusalem, beyond the borders of Samaria. The people living there were both Jewish and Gentile, so in a way, Galilee represented the world at large. Jesus began His ministry in "Galilee of the Gentiles," where "the people who sat in darkness have seen a great light" (Matt. 4:15–16 NKJV). Jesus would also give His Great Commission to the disciples in Galilee. From there He commanded them to "Go therefore and make disciples of all the nations" (Matt. 28:19 NKJV).

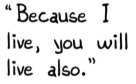

"Because I live, you will live also."

—John 14:19 NKJV

What Does It Mean?

The Resurrection of Jesus Christ is the single greatest event in the history of the world. It's so foundational to Christianity that no one who denies it can be a true Christian. Without the Resurrection there is no Christian faith, no salvation, and no hope. "If there is no resurrection of the dead," Paul explains, "then Christ is not risen. And if Christ is not risen, then our preaching is empty and your faith is also empty" (1 Cor. 15:13–14 NKJV). A person who believes in a Christ who was not raised believes in a powerless Christ, a dead Christ. And if Christ didn't rise from the dead, then no redemption was accomplished at the Cross and "your faith is futile," as Paul goes on to say; "you are still in your sins!" (1 Cor. 15:17 NKJV).

It's hardly surprising, then, that the first sermon on the day the church was born focused on the Resurrection of Christ. Peter declared the full gospel, beginning first with Christ's death and quickly testifying to the power of a resurrected Jesus, "whom God raised up, having loosed the pains of death, because it was not possible that He should be held by it" (Acts 2:24 NKJV).

Just as the Crucifixion is personally good news to each of us because of its redemptive meaning, the Resurrection is truly good news because of the *living* Christ, whose sacrifice made us clean. The two go hand-in-hand. The Resurrection is the power of the Cross, and the Cross is the meaning behind the Resurrection.

But it takes believing to receive the fruits of Jesus' amazing work. Christ made that clear throughout His ministry: "I am the way, the truth, and the life. No one comes to the Father except through Me" (John 14:6 NKJV). "Comes to the Father" means eternal life. In other words, entering into the eternal life that Jesus showed through His Resurrection takes *believing* in Him—believing that He is the Christ and that He was resurrected.

Paul says it this way: "If you confess with your mouth the Lord Jesus and believe in your heart that God has raised Him from the dead, you will be saved. For with the heart one believes unto righteousness, and with the mouth confession is made unto salvation" (Rom. 10:9–10 NKJV). Salvation is equal to eternal life, to deliverance from sin, and to eternal hope. Salvation determines a person's destiny in the presence of God in the glories of heaven forever. And salvation belongs only to those who believe in the Resurrection of Jesus Christ and who confess Him as Lord and Savior. To those He offers an eternal life of friendship with Him.

> The Resurrection of Jesus Christ is the single greatest event in the history of the world.

10. Have you entered into this relationship with Him and confessed it out loud? If not, what's keeping you from doing so?

_____

_____

_____

Jesus has already paid the price for your sins and simply asks that you believe in Him to gain the rewards. Why do you think so many people turn this down?

Wrapping It Up

Peter spoke of our "living hope through the resurrection of Jesus Christ from the dead, to an inheritance incorruptible and undefiled and that does not fade away, reserved in heaven for you" (1 Pet. 1:3–4 NKJV). In his vision on the island of Patmos, John saw the Lord Jesus Christ, who declared, "I am the First and the Last. I am He who lives, and was dead, and behold, I am alive forevermore" (Rev. 1:17–18 NKJV). The foundation of all our hope is expressed in Jesus' own words: "I am the resurrection and the life. He who believes in Me, though he may die, he shall live" (John 11:25 NKJV), and "Because I live, you will live also" (John 14:19 NKJV).

If Christ hadn't gone through the Passion, we'd still be sacrificing lambs just to be cleansed of our sin for the day. And if He hadn't risen from the dead, we'd be worshiping an awesome but nonetheless limited God. Instead, He went through both, and His Passion can now be our passion; His Resurrection, our resurrection. What a God!

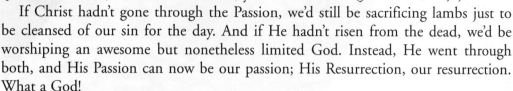

Things to Remember

- ❦ The women fully expected to find Jesus wrapped in His grave cloths and lying in the tomb.
- ❦ Just as they entered the garden, the women saw that the stone had already been rolled away from the entrance.
- ❦ Jesus hadn't needed to be unwrapped from the grave cloths that enveloped His body any more than He had needed to have the stone removed to leave the tomb. One moment He was encased in linen, and the next He was free.
- ❦ When Jesus called Mary by her name, she knew Him for who He was— the risen Christ.
- ❦ As the women stood in the presence of the risen Christ, their only response was to praise and adore Him.
- ❦ The first sermon on the day the church was born focused on the Resurrection of Christ.
- ❦ Salvation belongs only to those who believe in the Resurrection of Jesus Christ and who confess Him as Lord and Savior.

Memorize This!

*"I am the resurrection and the life. He who believes
in Me, though he may die, he shall live."*
—John 11:25 NKJV

Check This Out

If you want to find out more about the following related topics, check out John MacArthur's extensive resources in the *MacArthur LifeWorks Library CD-ROM*, or visit www.gty.org.

✚ The Sabbath
✚ The angels at the tomb
✚ The empty tomb
✚ The burial cloths
✚ The women's first encounter with Jesus
✚ Jesus' appearance in Galilee
✚ Hope through the Resurrection

Notes

THE MACARTHUR
SCRIPTURE MEMORY SYSTEM

JOHN MACARTHUR POURS HIS HEART into his work as a Bible teacher, and now he teaches Scripture, literally one verse at a time, with *The MacArthur Scripture Memory System*. The System comes in a turned-edge book, complete with the following timeless elements:

- 3 audio CDs with Dr. MacArthur reading the verse-of-the-week, and providing a brief statement of what that verse means and why it is so important to remember.

- A handy pack of printed cards, one for each verse, so that you can put one in your wallet or purse to refresh your memory of the weekly verse.

- CD-ROM containing a dynamic desktop complete with the text of each week's verse and a link to listen to the audio of the verse! Also contains a screen saver with each week's verse.

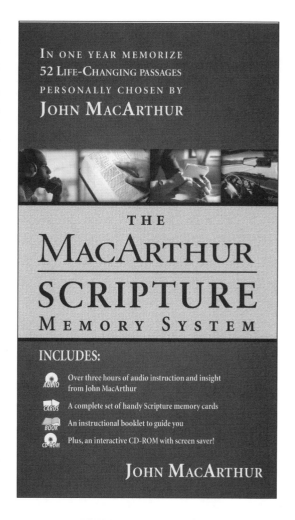

IN ONE YEAR MEMORIZE
52 LIFE-CHANGING PASSAGES
PERSONALLY CHOSEN BY
JOHN MACARTHUR

THE
MACARTHUR
SCRIPTURE
MEMORY SYSTEM

INCLUDES:

AUDIO   Over three hours of audio instruction and insight from John MacArthur

CARDS   A complete set of handy Scripture memory cards

BOOK   An instructional booklet to guide you

CD-ROM   Plus, an interactive CD-ROM with screen saver!

JOHN MACARTHUR

ISBN: 0-7852-5061-1

For old and new Bible readers alike, *The MacArthur Scripture Memory System* is an excellent way to really get into the Word and commit it to memory.

NELSON REFERENCE & ELECTRONIC
A Division of Thomas Nelson Publishers
Since 1798
www.thomasnelson.com